THE
JUST
MARKET

THE
JUST
MARKET

*Torah's Response
to the Crisis of the
Modern Economy*

JONATHAN BRANDOW

LANGDON STREET PRESS

Langdon Street Press
322 First Avenue N, 5th floor
Minneapolis, MN 55401
612.455.2293
www.langdonstreetpress.com

ISBN-13: 978-1-62652-831-4
LCCN: 2014937729

Distributed by Itasca Books

Book design by Kristeen Ott

Printed in the United States of America

To Rabbi Alexander Shapiro z"l, who inspired me.

CONTENTS

PREFACE

I was just a few years out of college when I hired on as a welder at the Fore River shipyard in Quincy, Massachusetts. Five thousand production employees worked at the yard, down from a World War II peak of about thirty thousand.

The welders and other trades were represented by Shipbuilders Local 5, a once-militant industrial union that had swept to power in the late thirties. The union had gone stale since the end of a long, vicious strike in the mid-sixties and then teetered on the edge of collapse after another in 1977, just a few months after I finished training. Years later, shipyard workers recalled the 1977 strike for two things: an infuriating lack of communication from the union leadership, and energetic race-baiting on the picket lines by the same bunch.

Irish- and Italian-American tradesmen dominated the work force. As many of them saw things, it was their yard by right. But by the mid-seventies, the tiny population of African-American, Cape Verdean, Caribbean, and Puerto Rican workers had swelled due to federal affirmative action laws. By the time I arrived, the welding, grinding, and shipfitting departments looked pretty much like the general population in the Boston metro area, or at least the male half of it. The relatively privileged trades—pipefitters, sheet metal workers, and others who were assigned to heated fabrication shops rather than the frigid (or sweltering) hulls of the ships under construction—remained virtually all white.

I spent my work hours welding and my spare time arguing with other activists over plans to revive a rank-and-file movement. It didn't take too many months on second shift to understand that the key to getting the average welder's vote wasn't the promise of higher wages; it was simple respect that everyone in the yard's largest and most pressured department longed for.

Three years after I started, I was elected as one of two welding department stewards, carried to victory by fourteen hundred young black and white welders fed up with an arrogant company and a deaf union. In 1982, I ran for and won the presidency of Local 5, then struggled in equal measure with the company and a union executive board dominated by officers of the old guard—over safety, over racially charged discipline, over abusive treatment, over forced overtime, over subcontractors. It often felt like I spent my final three years at the shipyard learning the meaning of the word "intractable." Regular "labor unrest" articles appeared in the *Boston Globe* and the *Quincy Patriot-Ledger*, including several on the mass suspensions and firings of more than fifty welders and, just a few years later, my own.

In its heyday, hundreds of Jewish tradesmen worked at the shipyard, streaming in from the urban enclaves of Mattapan and Lynn to the north. Thirty-five years later, I was one of a small handful of Jews plying a trade inside the gates. The majority were, like me, twentysomething rank-and-file "colonizers" who'd graduated from largely elite colleges and then chose the dry docks over a profession. Most of the activists weren't Jewish, but a disproportionately high percentage sure were.

I lived in Boston's run-down Fields Corner neighborhood. Although gospel music soared each Sunday morning from the Baptist church down the block from my house, the Hebrew inscription over the front door betrayed the building's former Jewish life. In all my shipyard years, that church was as close as I got to the inside of a synagogue.

And yet, I fasted on Yom Kippur. I sometimes lit candles on Friday night, the start of the Sabbath. And a few years into my time as a welder, I even hosted what was quite likely the first-ever shipyard Freedom Seder.

For me, it was about more than political residue from the sixties, though I shared plenty of that with the other shipyard progressives. But I'd also been involved with a campus group called the Radical Zionist Alliance and then moved on to construction work in an Israeli town for almost two years, hoping (unsuccessfully) to discover the meaning of the RZA slogan "Be a revolutionary in Zion and a Zionist in the Revolution."

Especially to readers who missed the sixties, that no doubt sounds bizarre. But the Jewish culture I'd absorbed as a child placed a higher value on political activism than it did on donations of either dollars or services to charity. My parents were more likely to join a fair housing council or hop a bus to an antiwar demonstration in Washington than contribute to the local food pantry. They were among the 15% of US Jews who voted for the Progressive Party in 1948—six times the level of Progressive support in the general population, and a significant chunk of the 90% of Jews who'd voted against the Republicans. In 1963, the rabbi of my childhood responded to a call by Abraham Joshua Heschel to go to Birmingham and stand with Martin Luther King, Jr. A photo of the three of them sat in my rabbi's office, impressing itself on my thirteen-year-old sensibility.

The walls of my three-day-a-week Hebrew school were festooned with posters of *chalutzim* (Zionist pioneers) and communal *kibbutzim*. No class was complete without a *pushke* (collection box) dedicated to the Zionist cause. I lived in a sedate Jewish pocket outside Philadelphia whose families were climbing the post-war economic ladder, but I had friends whose accountant fathers sent them to overnight camps linked to leftist political parties in Israel, a summer experience that modeled a Poconos version of kibbutz life.

I'd been brought up to understand that no matter where we found ourselves in the pecking order, social and economic justice advocacy was a Jewish civilizational ethic, the political equivalent of lox and a schmear. It was all very Exodus, very Prophets, very cloudy and distant. That mix somehow became the dominant influence on choices I'd make with the first half of my life.

This Jewish predilection for progressive advocacy was commonly recognized, though not entirely understood. And really, who could deny the kernel of free market economist Milton Friedman's bewilderment that Jews were not more grateful to capitalism despite their success with the system?[1] Or the wry observation of Milton Himmelfarb, the research director of the American Jewish Committee, that Jews tended to "earn like Episcopalians and vote like Puerto Ricans"?[2]

I won't say that those days are gone, but they've certainly faded. True, Jews still vote for liberals in high numbers. A white Jewish male earning more than $100,000 was 60% more likely to vote for Barack Obama in 2012 than a non-Jewish voter who matched his every other demographic characteristic. Income aside, Jews were 77% more likely than the average Caucasian voter to cast a ballot for Obama in his final campaign.[3] But the community passion for social and economic justice simply isn't what it was in the days when fully 38% of Jewish voters—*more than ten times the national proportion*—supported Eugene Debs and the Socialist Party.[4]

In 2004, sociologists Anna Greenberg and Kenneth D. Wald noted that by a two-to-one margin:

> ... participants in Jewish surveys ... define a "good" Jew as somebody who contributes to Jewish causes, supports civil rights for black Americans . . . and embraces other progressive social values . . . (F)or many Jews, the values of their religion are understood to promote attachment to a liberal political agenda carried into public life.[5]

I'm not sure that Greenberg and Wald's contention would find firm footing today. Jewish fundamentalists—including distinct ultra-Orthodox and ultra-nationalist segments—are increasingly prominent on the Jewish stage, both in Israel and the US. Jews may still be uncomfortable with the public face of right-wing politicians like Eric Cantor (or for that matter, Avigdor Lieberman, Naftali Bennet, and Moshe Feiglin in Israel) and moneymen like Sheldon Adelson. But the extremist Cantors and Adelsons really just create space for more modulated Jewish conservatives like Dan Senor, Ari Fleischer, Dennis Prager, and even David Brooks, none of whom are any longer the odd Jew out, but rather celebrated, highly paid media talking heads with Jewish public personas. The 2012 US election cycle even witnessed the transformation of celebrity Rabbi Shmuley

Boteach into a Republican politician who espoused "family values" while distorting the Jewish economic justice agenda into a celebration of the free market.[6] This rightist leadership bid, and the increased support of Jews for Republicans and other conservative candidates, are indicative of inroads into the perception of "Jewish values"—a tendency that mimics the efforts of gentile religious conservatives who have successfully altered the American political discourse over the last thirty years. The majority of Jews haven't yet parked on that end of the political spectrum, but in Jewish Time (late as ever) things seem to be swinging that way.

Sixty percent of US Jews still agree that the government should "do more" to help needy Americans. But only 32% feel that "government … should see to it that every person has a job and a good standard of living." Only 28% now think that it's government's job to undo the legacy of discrimination and "make every effort to improve the social and economic position of blacks."[7]

But economic policy isn't the focus of the new Jewish Right, which instead promotes two core issues of its own. The first is a conservative social outlook near and dear to the most traditional religious communities (think homophobia and outlawed abortion). The second, a Greater Israel orientation, is aggressively pursued by messianic Zionists in Israel and by secular American Jews in search of a tribalist rallying point that feeds their sense of belonging. There's no evidence that either tendency is supported by a Jewish majority. Nor does either account for the apparently weakened economic policy values that had been synonymous with modern Jewish life—and whose foundations stretch back to Torah and Talmud.

So why have the economic and social justice values of Jews dissipated, seemingly over the course of only a generation or two?

Historian Jerry Z. Muller suggests that Jews who are "consciously or tacitly aware of the antipathy brought on by their success" create defense mechanisms by advocating for disadvantaged social classes.[8] As examples of those defenses, he cites "conspicuous" philanthropy to the "culture and social welfare of the larger (non-Jewish) community" as well as the promotion of governmental income transfers.[9] Muller's conclusion implies that, given historical opportunity, Jews will abandon self-protective mechanisms and blend into the self-interested woodwork of other economically advantaged communities.

It's certainly true that economically successful Jews no longer perceive the need for "protection" from envious segments of the gentile population simply because of their relative "Jewish" wealth. And, for the first time since the Great Depression, significant numbers of Jews (though still a minority of them) are voting and acting on behalf of their personal financial interests rather than Jewish values—that is to say, for their individual benefit rather than the social good.

That seems to align with Muller's hypothesis, but his materialist argument doesn't completely satisfy, largely because it obscures the struggle taking place in the modern Jewish sensibility between a progressive ethos and the pressures of individualism. That ethos is rooted in advocacy for the weak and disenfranchised, not as a purely religious value, but as a human imperative that extends beyond any individual level of religious adherence—tailor-made, one would suppose, for secularized modern Jewry. Identifying perhaps the earliest example of that ethos, James Diamond, the chair of Jewish Studies at the University of Waterloo, characterizes the killing of the Egyptian taskmaster in Exodus like this:

Moses sacrifices his promising future among the very upper echelons of the ruling class and risks death, not for the sake of God or religion, but for the sake of another human being.[10]

A stark undercurrent of class and national subjugation lurks behind the biblically sanctioned killing. The risk of a man's privilege and future prospects are outweighed by the call of justice. It's all about man-to-man, not man-to-God.

And here's what's changing: Modern Jews and gentiles alike rest relatively easily with the freedoms of others who "do no harm" to their personal lives. For Jews, these issues are win-win; gender equality and gay rights, for example, are socially just and by their nature shore up the rights of other potentially targeted populations. To be clear: I support those rights and have for a very long time. But there's a problem: instead of *amplifying* the Jewish economic justice ethos, these and similar concerns are increasingly *substituted* for it. When social equity concerns wade into serious economic waters, raising the specter of a zero-sum game, individual self-interest takes a toll.

Writing about the contemporary drift toward individualism in the larger US society, commentator Kurt Andersen notes that

> ... extreme individualism has been triumphant ... A kind of tacit grand bargain was forged ... Going forward, the youthful masses of every age would be permitted as never before to indulge their self-expressive and hedonistic impulses. But capitalists in return would be unshackled as well, free to

indulge . . . with fewer and fewer fetters in the forms of regulation, taxes, or social opprobrium.[11]

With freedom, as the saying goes, comes responsibility. But avoiding responsibility can be so alluring—and so lucrative! Every fiber of the endless opportunity and privatization of Western life presses toward abandoning the social ethics of the heritage. And it is precisely the issues that surround "extreme individualism"—including greed and questionable business practices—that most insidiously dilute the historical economic justice values of the Jewish community.

It is truly remarkable that, in the face of these pressures and the deterioration of traditional Jewish community ties, Jewish progressivism remains a force at all. And yet, as late as 2012, the Public Religion Research Institute found that 76% of all Jews (and 80% of those who believe that the pursuit of social justice is important) want synagogues to advocate for public policies. An even higher percentage of synagogue-affiliated Jews (83%) felt the same way.[12]

While some think that politics has no place in a religious community, Jewish history, like all national histories, is chock-full of ideological sparring that represents different visions of the past and different roads to the national future. In the era of the second Temple, the violent fanaticism of the Zealots and Sicarii played a significant role in bringing down the wrath of the Romans on Jerusalem. In the late nineteenth and early twentieth centuries, Yiddish headlines were aflame with the conflicts between the European Jewish labor movement and the emerging Jewish small capitalist class.[13] Later, sometimes-violent clashes among Zionist factions reflected disagreements over strategy and tactics in the pre-state struggle against British colonialism. Especially in the two countries in which modern Jewry has the most significant political impact—the US and Israel—Jewish political views are no less a bellwether of our direction as a people.

And so, if the progressive Jewish tradition really has legitimate roots, and has demonstrated a powerful hold on Jews over time, how could that part of our culture become so weakened by the pressures of modern individualism so quickly? I'll suggest two culprits: Jewish institutional leadership and the Jewish Left.

Rabbinical leadership routinely sidesteps economic justice issues under the guise of keeping partisan politics out of religion—what Rabbi Sharon Kleinbaum bleakly characterizes as "boring, safe religious leadership."[14] Perhaps that's why rabbinical sermons often delve into social issues like gender equality or gay marriage but tend to steer away from wage gaps, affirmative action, or even the rights of undocumented immigrants. Instead, synagogue social action committees offer a menu of food pantry collections and Habitat for Humanity days. There's no question that worthy charitable endeavors service the poor, and well-designed efforts like Habitat or Dress for Success encourage recipients to help themselves out of poverty. But in general, most synagogue "social action" as currently conceived does little to effect social change—certainly not at a policy level.

The choice of community leadership to stand silent about what even constitutes "Jewish economic policy" leaves the vast majority of modern Jews without a Jewish guide to our times. Affiliated Jews are left rudderless and the unaffiliated increasingly disaffected. Without leadership that *calls on Jews to discern and act on behalf of historical values with which many still sympathize*, the unaffiliated 50% will be disinclined to pursue its already tenuous links with Jewish life. With the erosion of the ethical leg of what the socialist-Zionist ideologue Dov Ber Borochov termed "the visioned common historic past,"[15] *the Jewish majority is stranded without a vision for our times.* And here the Ancients had it right: "Without vision, the people becomes chaotic" (Proverbs 29:18).[16]

Those who actively identify as progressive Jews—as I do—are also at fault. Many of us—again, like me—have been content to prioritize contemporary politics and never get past those gauzy connections to the Prophets or Exodus. We have never articulated exactly how our heritage is connected to difficult modern issues of economic justice. But if the influence of a Jewish progressive culture is to be rebuilt, it's up to people like me to demonstrate how our politics are rooted in Torah ethics, are informed by the observations and methodology of the tradition, and can be applied to the context of modern social and political life. No one else—no traditional Torah scholars, no rabbinate dependent on the goodwill of a handful of well-to-do congregants—is going to do it.

In 1934, the leading journalist of the labor Zionist movement in pre-state Palestine called on the Jewish people to extract ancient ethics from the archives of their civilization and apply them to modernity. Berl Katznelson suggested that it was time to "descend into ruined grottoes, to excavate the dust from that which had laid in forgetfulness, to resuscitate traditions which have the power to stimulate the generation of renewal."[17] His words were echoed seventy years later by *New York Times* columnist Frank Bruni, who observed that meaningful adaptations of religion-based values must be

... more than reflexive fidelity to chosen passages from ancient writings. They hinge on the human intellect and its ability to filter timeless values through modern understanding.[18]

Bruni was critiquing Tea Party darling-of-the-moment Michele Bachmann. Katznelson spoke to a four-thousand-year-old tradition of social justice and freedom that is crucial to the foundations of the Jewish people. Let's be wise enough to listen.

The approach I take in this book will, I hope, speak to those of any religion or nationality who agree that society might be improved by transmitting values of economic justice that have endured from generation to generation and still resonate with contemporary sensibilities. The biblical roots of the values discussed in *The Just Market* will likely be familiar not only to Jews, but also to Christians who grasp the historical context within which Jesus of Nazareth lived and spoke. While Jewish texts form the basis for this book, and Jews clearly comprise the primary audience, it's obvious that from a historical perspective, Christian sources not only have something to say about Torah values, but also serve as witness to the context and application of the Law to Jewish life in the period that led to the rise of rabbinical Judaism, the codification of the Oral Law, and the development of the Talmud. I hope and believe that Christian progressives, in addition to Jews, might find value and comfort in the discussion that follows.

INTRODUCTION TO
THE JUST MARKET

The Just Market Concept

Torah and Talmud point to a set of economic values that, viewed as a whole, comprise a guide to equitable, balanced social policies—even in the modern age. I term the framework presented by those values "The Just Market."

The purpose of the Just Market is to assure a reasonable level of prosperity for all social strata. Individual wealth creation is one tool in the Just Market kit. But so are social balance and the incentives of personal satisfaction, creativity, and social responsibility.

Of course, ancient values are no more than curiosities unless they respond to contemporary social and economic concerns. The values of the Just Market do just that. Their substance and implications for current economic policy and action are the focus of this book.

While its source documents are based on religious beliefs reaching back to Sinai, the Just Market is not inherently theological. It does not argue for an economic theocracy. It makes room for, but does not require, belief in a divine entity. It welcomes, but does not require, spirituality.

In the place of an articulated framework, Just Market source texts include religious commandments and commentaries that present ancient legal cases, rabbinical opinions, and guidance around what we would today term social policy, commercial ethics, and market practices. In some cases, religious discussion that appears focused on another subject entirely is adapted to clarify economic values of the Ancients that might otherwise be obscure to the contemporary reader. Sometimes, these metaphors also serve as uncomfortable reminders of the prejudices of our forefathers; the Talmudic case of a bride with a hidden blemish, for example, is eventually applied to the laws of commercial fraud, analogizing "property" of very different sorts.[19]

Anachronisms notwithstanding, the Just Market perspective derives from biblical sources that likely originated almost three millennia ago and evolved substantially over a period of more than two thousand years. How we understand the context in which those values were formed naturally influences the attempt to apply them to current concerns. This introduction comments on three aspects of that background: the historical development of those values, the Jewish yearning for a vision of the ideal society, and the place of values-based advocacy in the development of Jewish tradition. The guts of this book are found in the six chapters that examine the foundations of the Just Market outlook. Each of these chapters concludes with a summary and action bullets with the heading From Ethics to Advocacy.

An appendix notes contending Jewish approaches to economic policy issues. Another provides a brief look at the links between selected sections of the Christian Testament and Just Market values.

The Road to the Just Market

The first Temple of the Israelites was built by King Solomon, son of David, and was operated by a caste of priests from the tribe of Levi. After Solomon's death in 931 BCE, the Kingdom of Judea splintered and a new Kingdom of Israel formed in the north. The Davidic empire was reduced to the southern tribal territories, including Jerusalem. The Temple caste, which had controlled religious life from its center in David's capital, was weakened by the split, but remained intact with the Temple operation at its core.

A little more than two hundred years later, conquering Assyrians liquidated the northern kingdom and dispersed its population, originating the mythology surrounding the Ten Lost Tribes. Judea maintained sovereignty for another 350 years before the Persians exiled the Jewish intelligentsia to Babylon in modern-day Iraq and then destroyed the Jerusalem Temple.

The Jews were permitted to return to Judea some fifty years later, but many stayed in Babylon. The repatriated leadership led the reconstruction of a modest second Temple in Jerusalem, which survived the transition to Greek rule during the reign of Alexander the Great. In general, the priestly caste and its supporters (called Sadducees) claimed authority that came directly from the "revealed law" of Torah, which they alone transmitted and secured through control of the Temple rituals. The Sadducees belittled the interpretative basis of what was known as the Oral Law (*Torah b'al peh*), since it opened the way for the rise of competing leaderships.

The Oral Law expanded on the many cryptic commands and passages in Torah that urged a lifestyle based on divine vision. Torah had initially laid out laws of human conduct for a settled environment that superseded that of the twelve wandering Hebrew tribes. Later, the prophets spoke to Judeans and Israelites living in sovereign Jewish polities. As the social and economic framework of Jewish life evolved, including submission to Babylonian, Greek, and then Roman rule, corresponding adaptations of the law that could be applied to everyday life assumed new urgency.

In the aftermath of the Maccabean revolt against the Greeks in 165 BCE (the event that forms the basis of the Chanukah holiday) an alternative religious sect, the Pharisees, began to take form. The Pharisees differed from the Sadducees on two issues important to the subject at hand. They believed in an afterlife, which they called *olam ha'bah*, or "the world-to-come," an existence of perfect justice. And they affirmed the legitimacy of ongoing human interpretation of Torah, which they promoted through the Oral Law.

Even where Torah became abruptly specific—in its detailed instructions on how to use weights in commercial transactions, for example—the means of implementation were often ambiguous. Most Torah texts concerning economic and market issues merely paint a background of broad ethical practices toward unwary consumers and communities. Its basic commercial guidelines usually require significant clarification. For example, "You shall not insult the deaf or place a stumbling block before the blind" (Leviticus 19:14); "When you sell property to your neighbor, or buy any from your neighbor, you shall not wrong one another" (Leviticus 25:14); or even the slightly more specific "You shall not move your neighbor's landmarks" (Deuteronomy 19:14) were all unenforceable without further iteration.

As early exponents, the Prophets were preachers, not lawmakers, who tended to speak in two modes. Their rhetorical style often captured the spirit of economic justice, as in Isaiah's call to "untie the cords of the yoke, to let the oppressed go free" (Isaiah 58:6, read each Yom Kippur) or Amos's impassioned demand to "let justice well up like water" (Amos 5:24). Today, general pleas for justice like these are more commonly highlighted than the more pointed prophetic opposition to monopolists who "add house to house and join field to field" (Isaiah 5:8) or condemnations of those who "use an *ephah* (weight) that is too small, and a *shekel* that is too big, tilting a dishonest scale" (Amos 8:5).[20] It's not taking anything away from them to say that the Prophets were lyrically strong but short on the mechanics of implementation.

Rabbi Joseph Telushkin notes that Torah text requires interpretation and mitigation, since the literal laws are stated in extreme language for poetic effect:

> The Written Law, for example, demands an "eye for an eye" (Exodus 21:24). Did this imply that if one person accidentally blinded another, he should be blinded in return? . . . (T)he Oral Law explains that the verse must be understood as requiring monetary compensation: the value of an eye is what must be paid.[21]

Spurred by historic necessity, the breadth and acceptance of interpreted Torah grew after the appearance of the Pharisee sect. The tide shifted decisively when the Romans crushed the Judean rebellion that began in the year 66 of the Common Era (CE). An estimated one hundred thousand Jews were killed in the siege of Jerusalem over the next four years; many times that number were enslaved or exiled. In 70 CE, the Romans destroyed the second Temple, disrupting Jewish national life and threatening the basis of the entire religious civilization. The *raison d'etre* of the temple caste was erased. The priests and their Sadducee supporters effectively disappeared.

As the only coherent Jewish leadership after the destruction of Jerusalem, the Pharisees developed a mission to preserve the knowledge and common application of the Oral Law. Their movement grew into the early form of rabbinic Judaism, emerging at the end of the first century of the Common Era as the authoritative guide to personal and commercial life. The place of the Oral Law in the national structure was sealed when it was codified as the *Mishnah* under the guidance of Rabbi Judah Hanasi around 220 of the Common Era.

The Mishnah was supplemented by two major commentaries over the next four hundred years. The rabbinical community between the Tigris and the Euphrates rivers developed the Babylonian Talmud, the dominant legal work of Jewish civilization, while rabbis based in Palestine wrote the Jerusalem Talmud, which paid more attention to issues specific to the historic territory of the Jews. Through these texts, the Ancients adapted Torah to generate a powerful guide to ethical life, including business conduct and the rules of the marketplace.

The Vision of Zion

After the final Roman exile transformed the Jewish nation from a sovereign people to a landless one, the rabbinate responded with a messianic vision that would nurture Jewish civilization for two thousand years. Instead of a stone temple in Jerusalem that fulfilled the literal command of the divinity, Judaism would center on the creation of a perfect Zion of the heart and mind, yet maintain the centrality of its tie to the land of Israel.

This vision of Zion floated between real and ideal worlds. The relationship of Diaspora populations to the actual territory of Zion included frequent pilgrimages and, less often, return to the homeland; charitable contributions to Zion's increasingly destitute Jews; and intellectual exchange, including the development of visions for the longed-for national meeting point of a dispersed people. Yehuda Kurtzer summarizes the historical interaction as described by the ancient Alexandrian Jewish philosopher Philo around 20 BCE this way:

> . . . a "mother-city" (Jerusalem) to which satellite communities (such as Philo's Alexandria) felt a familial relationship; a legacy of pilgrimage and philanthropy towards the metropolis; and the ancient synagogue as a gathering place to reaffirm the centrality of shared peoplehood even in faraway lands.[22]

In the visionary realm, discourse over how the perfect Zion would engage the world—should it ever materialize—stretched over millennia. The discussion was untroubled by the fact that the Jews controlled neither a sovereign state nor a unified territory.

One of these exchanges concerned, of all things, the conduct of sovereign war. Here was a discussion authored by representatives of a powerless people, living under a variety of foreign rulers and with no existing or foreseeable military apparatus. Yet the rabbis who codified the Oral Law two hundred

years after the destruction of the Jewish commonwealth discussed
who could make the decision to go to war;[23] the differences in
the nature and conduct of obligatory and voluntary wars;[24] and
sexual violence on the battlefield.[25] Almost fifty generations later,
leading rabbis—Moses Maimonides of Egypt and Morocco,
Moses ben Nakhman Girondi of Spain, and Rabbi Shlomo Yitz-
khaki of France (commonly known as Rashi)—continued the
same conversation, detailing ethical policies and behaviors for a
(still nonexistent) Jewish state.[26]

These commentators debated values and laws that would
never have any political effect without radical, unlikely changes in
the national condition.[27] Their only possible purpose was to articulate religiously based policy and ethics that bound the Jewish
people to a common vision of the future. Theological underpin-
nings aside, this was—like Moses slaying the Egyptian taskmaster—about relations between nation and nation, not man and
divinity. In the same vein, Jewish civilization expended tremen-
dous intellectual resources detailing policies for the conduct of an
ethical and socially just market.

Jews did not, of course, live in perfect communities. If there
had been no fraudulent behavior, intricate laws to protect against
it would not have been needed. If hoarding and speculation had
not been real threats to the social fabric, laws to shield Jewish
communities from those practices would not have appeared.

Although Jews considered the development of the law
part of the quest toward a godly society, they also understood that
the ideal world would always be beyond their grasp. The Talmudic
Sage Samuel contended that "the only difference between this
world and the days of the messiah is the exile of Israel among the
nations."[28] That is to say, during the messianic era the Jews could

expect to regain sovereignty over their lives and their historical homeland. But injustice would not disappear of its own accord.

The Ancients deduced that if the messianic era would not herald the perfect society, then Jews were saddled with the infinite task of imagining, advocating, and constructing a just world. To build that elusive society, it had to be envisioned first. And so, that visioning process became integral to the writings of Jewish commentators seeking to explain Torah and Mishnah in the context of individual and collective Jewish responsibilities in the world. The result was the Talmud. The foundations of the Just Market emerge from those efforts.

So who were these guys, anyway?

Some proponents of Jewish tradition would later imbue the Ancients with almost papal infallibility. But although personal experience and station were not by themselves determining factors in Talmudic discussion, each commentator would certainly have evaluated the texts through a personal lens that reflected his individual outlook and background; otherwise we would probably not have inherited the level of disputation that Talmud presents.

Some Sages were born into wealth and held significant business interests during their lives. One of these, Rav Khiyya bar Yosef, was a salt wholesaler whose infrequent opinions in commercial cases were so colored by his own financial interests that other rabbis threatened him with "the curse of the Sages."[29] On the other end of the spectrum, the similarly named Rav Khiyya bar Abba was an itinerant teacher who was forced to leave Palestine due to financial difficulties. Rav Yokhana bar Nafkha was an orphan whose father died before his birth and his mother soon after. Resh Lekish was a bandit and gladiator before turning to Torah. And as Hershey Friedman, director of business

programs at Brooklyn College writes, most Talmudic commentators depended upon common secular occupations, "such as beer
brewer, farmer, farm worker, peddler, physician, wood chopper,
merchant, blacksmith, gravedigger."[30]

These typically checkered life experiences among
Talmudic-era commentators naturally flavor the exchanges in
which the Ancients engaged. The lens through which each inter-
prets Torah principles would differ from teacher to teacher. Similarly, there would be differences in the application of law and
justice from place to place, community to community, situation
to situation.

That level of flexibility is reflected in Talmud's insistence
on context in the interpretation and application of economic
law. As one result, there's no straight line from Torah to the Just
Market—nor to any interpretation of the source texts, for that
matter. In fact, the texts often portray ideological contention no
less heated than that between MoveOn and the Tea Party (or, in
an Israeli context, between Meretz and Yisrael Beiteinu) today.

Belief and Behavior

As the drama at Sinai builds to a climax, Torah tells us that God
is enraged by the abomination of the golden calf. God threatens
to destroy the people Israel, ordering Moses to step aside so that
"my anger may blaze forth against them, and that I may destroy
them" (Exodus 32:10).

But Moses doesn't flinch. If Israel is destroyed, he warns,
God will be mocked as a fool and a liar among the peoples of the
world as the god who promised redemption only to annihilate his
own chosen when the selection proved to be iffy.

I, for one, sense a quiver in Rav Abbahu's voice as he reflects on this audacity:

> Were it not explicitly written, it would be impossible to say such a thing; that Moses took hold of the Holy One, blessed be He, like a man who seizes his fellow by his garment and said before Him: Sovereign of the Universe, I will not let go until You forgive and pardon them.[31]

Read literally, this is a powerful image. Read figuratively, the drama is no less stunning. In the ancient world, destiny ruled. Gods determined the past and the future. Gods dictated the fate of each person, of every tribe and people. When disaster descended, when nations triumphed, or if change of any sort occurred, one god or another got the credit. Yet in two sentences, Moses confounds the wisdom of all prior ages and religions. He takes action independent of God's will. God relents. Israel is saved.

A short time later, Torah is delivered to the tribes gathered at the foot of the mountain. Each Jew shoulders the responsibility to act on values derived from Torah. At that moment, the people themselves become makers of history. The way is paved for the codified Mishnah to confirm, more than a thousand years later, that "you are not obligated to complete the work, but neither are you free to desist from it."[32] And because Torah invokes a communal obligation, the Jewish collective from that point assumes a national responsibility to apply those values to the construction of a just world.

Despite the strong personal aspect of that commitment, the essence of the law is political. No individual can assure that "the same rule shall apply to you and to the stranger who resides among you" (Numbers 15:16). No individual can "appoint magistrates and clerks for your tribes, in all the settlements" (Deuteronomy 16:18). No individual can implement the system of market commissioners that Jewish law took from those texts, policing for fraud, unfair competitive practices, price-gouging, and runaway profit margins. No individual can create employment opportunity for all. Those responsibilities fit within a social structure of economic justice reflected by the values of the Just Market.

The Six Foundations of the Just Market

The express purpose of the classic free market paradigm is to provide a structure for the creation of individual wealth. Solely as a by-product of the pursuit of material wealth, prosperity may (or may not) flow beyond those who capitalize its creation.

Like the free market, Just Market values support the quest for competitive success. But the Just Market moderates individual desires with social responsibilities that go far beyond the classic free market social safety net or its surrogate, voluntary charity.

The Ancients designed law that encouraged competition while protecting the lower rungs on society's economic ladder. They developed policy that articulated deep respect for the value of labor and the people who undertake it. They even tried to balance economic growth with community impacts.

Of course, those same Ancients could not have envisioned how modernity might challenge their economic vision. They failed to imagine the use of capital as a tool to generate growth. In their zeal to maintain community stability, they leaned toward protectionism. In some cases they restricted competition while glossing over issues like product differentiation or consumer choice that obviously loom larger today than in ancient eras.

Although their program was constrained by the economic limitations of their times, many of the values they integrated into that earlier reality still resonate. Those values suggest an economic reorientation that differs radically from capitalist models in the US, Israel, and other westernized democracies.

That program can be broadly summarized as the Six Foundations of the Just Market:

- Access to the necessities of life
- Universal employment opportunity
- A level playing field
- Commercial and promotional integrity
- Respect for labor
- Sabbatical values

The first—universal access to the necessities of life—is essentially the Just Market mission, while the others represent either tools toward its achievement, values that condition it, or both.

A few notes on format:

Going forward, biblical citations in the text body are in traditional formats. Talmudic references cite the Babylonian Talmud. With a few exceptions to enhance readability, Talmudic references are noted with "BT" followed by the tractate and folio number, which roughly serves as a traditional page reference. Citations from the Mishnah are noted, along with the name of the relevant tractate. References to the Sages or the Ancients are traditional denotations for the rabbinical commentators whose discussions are enshrined in the Talmud. Other citations are generally left to the endnotes.

Unless otherwise specified, citations from the Jewish Testament are from the three-volume series *The Five Books of Moses-Prophets-Writings: A New Translation of the Holy Scriptures* published by the Jewish Publication Society of America (1962). Talmudic translations are from the *Soncino Talmud* (1934), and Christian Testament quotations in Appendix B are from *The Holy Bible: The New King James Version* published by Thomas Nelson (1982).

Throughout, references are made to the opinions of noted economists and commentators on current economic issues. Part of my motivation is, of course, to demonstrate that it's reasonable to adapt and apply Just Market values to modern economic and social concerns, and that the views of recognizable experts tend to mirror those values. While this is, in my opinion, the case, I do not imply that any of the individuals I cite agree with my theses, connect any of their positions to Just Market values, or are even aware of them.

Finally, note that totals in tables found throughout the book may not sum due to rounding.

The Six Foundations of the Just Market

Foundation 1—Access to the Necessities of Life: The Just Market promotes the opportunity for every person to access the necessities of life. It employs necessary regulatory tools to ensure that access, as well as social stability.

Foundation 2—Universal Employment Opportunity: The Just Market promotes universal employment opportunity through a series of social policy mechanisms and mandated set-asides.

Foundation 3—A Level Playing Field: The Just Market advocates for a level economic playing field that creates the broadest access to life's necessities and recognizes the needs of disadvantaged sectors and groups.

Foundation 4—Commercial and Promotional Integrity: The Just Market incentivizes ethical conduct and honest disclosure in market relationships. It condemns fraud in all its commercial and social forms, including character fraud practiced for monetary gain or power.

Foundation 5—Respect for Labor: The Just Market demands and rewards honest, respectful relations between employer and employee.

Foundation 6—Sabbatical Values: The Just Market advocates cyclical refreshment of the economic playing field, including alleviation of debt, the release of indentures both formal and informal, and the creation of a system of fair transgenerational transfers.

1. ACCESS TO THE NECESSITIES OF LIFE

At the end of the day, the primary purpose of the Just Market is to provide the opportunity for every member of society to access the "necessities of life," the most common translation of the Talmudic language *d'varim sheyesh ba'hen khayay nefesh*.

Jewish commentators over the centuries have discussed the implications of that phrase. But in virtually every case the Ancients applied tools—among them profit constraints, price regulation, and prohibitions on speculation—to moderate market behavior and promote access to "necessities" in the interests of the majority.

Nourishing "the Life of the Body and Soul"

A social understanding of the "necessities of life" of course varies with every civilization. Each modern environment produces its own "necessities" and develops tools to promote their attainment.

This Talmudic passage describes a set of necessities within the context of a discussion of hoarding, which may explain the relatively narrow nature of the items that are listed. The Sage Rav notes ("for instance") that the list itself is illustrative only:

> Fruit and things which are life's necessities as, for instance, wines, oils and the various kinds of flour, must not be hoarded; but spices, cumin and pepper may be. (BT Bava Batra 90b)

About a thousand years later, Maimonides explicitly called for profit constraints that facilitated popular access to necessities *of which examples only are given*:

> This (profit constraint) . . . applies only to articles that are necessities of life, *such as* wines, oils, and various kinds of flour. For spices such as costus root, frankincense, and the like, one may make as much profit as he desires. (Maimonides, *Laws of Sale* 14:2, italics added)[33]

Like Rav, Maimonides's use of the term "such as" indicates that his examples of necessities of life are just that. The contrasting luxuries he lists—"spices such as costus root, frankincense, and the like"—are examples as well. The language of the text aside, how do we know that these necessities are examples, not etched in stone but illustrations of the writers of different epochs? *Because they present different lists.* Earlier, the Mishnah iterates an even larger array of items subject to market price regulations, including grain, grapes, olives, fertilizer (also used as fuel), and construction materials and clay used for storage, housewares, and decorative products. (Mishnah Bava Metzia 5:7).

The ancient market was mainly a self-sufficient community—especially in terms of "necessities." Foreign commercial exchange was often luxury based. Costus root seems to have been either a fragrant herb or a form of ginger, probably African in origin. Frankincense is an aromatic resin with origins in Yemen. Thus, the reference to costus and frankincense is to spices and scents originating in far-flung regions—exotic products beyond the necessities of life. Maimonides makes no mention of fruit of any sort. The Sages use cumin as an example of a non-necessary luxury; Maimonides uses frankincense. Plainly, the iteration of "necessities" is subject to alteration depending on the writer, the times, and the role of the specific product in context.

The Ancients' understanding of the economic process was too sophisticated to imagine that they would have considered eggs a necessity, for example (Bava Batra 90a, 91a), but not the apparatus surrounding their production, which might have an even greater impact than would regulation on the price of the end product. So if eggs are included, what about hens, the roosters that sire them, the corn they are fed, and the pens in which they nest? Surely unrestrained profits on any raw materials or ancillary services ripple forward until pricing of the necessary product soars.

Likewise, it seems unlikely that the Ancients would have classified foodstuffs as necessities, but not clothing (or at least hides and fabrics) in a region where winters bring cold rains and, in the Galilee, Jerusalem, and northern Babylon, even snow—and where the onset of darkness in the south is accompanied by precipitous drops in temperature. In characterizing basic goods that Jews were obligated to offer to the poor, the oppressed, and the stranger, Torah poetically identifies clothing and bread as emblematic needs (Deuteronomy 10:18–19). And if woven fabric and hides are included, what about the looms that produced them or the sheep that provided the fleece?

That logic, which would have been apparent to the Ancients, suggests that the "necessities of life" meant something more than food staples. The language of Talmud itself provides additional evidence when it refers to the necessities as *d'varim sheyesh ba'hen khayay nefesh*, or "things within which are found the life of a being" (BT Bava Batra 89b). The text speaks of "things" (*d'varim*) which are in no way limited to foods (*okhel*). The recipient of these essential "things" is not a *goof* (body), nor a *n'shama*, commonly translated as "soul." Instead, the Ancients elected to use the word "*nefesh*," a word that straddles the material and spiritual aspects of life.

The complex meaning of the word "nefesh" is evident throughout the tradition. In the first book of Torah, the patriarch Jacob's trusted son Judah reacts to the possibility that his youngest brother might be held hostage by Joseph (who has not yet revealed himself as the outcast owner of the Coat of Many Colors from years before). Anticipating his father Jacob's reaction if he is forced to tell the old man that Benjamin, like the young Joseph, has been lost, Judah uses the possessive form of the word (*nafsho*) to indicate a complex of spiritual or emotional needs with a physical consequence:

> Now if I come to your servant my father, and the boy is not with us—since his own life is so bound up with his (*nafsho k'shura b'nafsho*)—when he sees that the boy is not with us he will die… (Genesis 44:30-31)

Here "nefesh" clearly connotes something more than food; rather, it describes the nuanced interplay of human needs that make the difference between a man who flourishes and one who withers. The same concept, using precisely the same phrase, is also used to describe the intimate bond between Jonathan and David, perhaps a thousand years later (1 Samuel 18:1).

With this background, it's reasonable to ask: Would a culture that has sustained itself for four thousand years really conclude that the sum total of "things" that nurture the life of the body and soul consists solely of food commodities? Unlikely.

Many years ago, I worked ten hours a day for twenty-five Israeli lira (about six dollars at the time), manually mixing concrete and greasing crude wooden forms that grew floor by floor into four-story, sixteen-unit walk-up apartments. The Palestinians laboring alongside me earned even less, and much of that was spent on transport from Gaza and back every day. At lunch—the day's only break from work—they chewed on a single peppery leaf laid flat in a pita. Our ten-hour workday stretched into sixteen for them before they were home, went to sleep, and at 4:00 a.m. began the trip back to the work site in Bat-Yam, then a small town south of Tel Aviv. By the most narrow definition, yes, they had the necessities of life, but hardly the resources to nurture their families or fully participate in a community. My own privileged background permitted me to walk off to another life at will; no one who worked next to me was as lucky.

Saving a Life

Does health care qualify as a "necessity of life"? The Talmud captures the priority of lifesaving efforts: "Whoever saves a life, it is as if he saved an entire world" (BT Sanhedrin 37a). This passage does not differentiate between heroic acts and routine medical caregiving. But routine care, not a unique act of heroism, is most often what "saves a life." The Ancients themselves analogized health care to what they saw as the Torah's unparalleled role as a life-imbuing agent: "To those who go to the right hand (of Torah), it is a medicine of life." (BT Shabbat 88b). On its face, then, health care rises to the level of life's necessities and is included in the category of lifesaving acts.

Why, then, in their discussion of "things within which are found the life of a being," would the Ancients fail to mention health care and list foods as examples instead? Possibly because foods were a key component of medical care as well as daily sustenance. In an epoch of primitive medical science, herbs, roots, and prescriptive day-to-day nutrients were the most common medicines, as Talmudic discussions of various remedies attest:

> Said Samuel: An open wound is to be regarded as dangerous for which the Sabbath may be profaned . . . For stopping the bleeding, cress with vinegar; for bringing on (flesh), scraped root of cynodon and the paring of the bramble . . . Said Rav Safra: A berry-like excrescence is a forerunner of the Angel of Death. What is the remedy for it? Rue in honey, or parsley in strong wine. (BT Avodah Zarah 28a)

Indeed, wine, which is among the Talmud's enumerated examples of life necessities, is extolled as a symbol of medicine and so, of life itself. Here wine is counterposed to the death-head of blood:

"At the head of all death am I, Blood: At the head
of all life am I, Wine." (How can that be?) . . .
What should be written is this: "At the head of all
sickness am I, Blood; at the head of all medicine
am I, Wine." (BT Bava Batra 58b)

Access to health care is required for life. Its delivery falls
within the same Talmudic parameters as other necessary goods
and services—and would be subject to the same regulatory tools
as other wholesale providers of necessities, which are discussed in
the sections Price Regulation and A Reasonable Profit Standard
later in this chapter.

How might we frame the "necessities of life" today? Food,
health care and adequate shelter would be included, of course, but
so might the means to survive in a technology-driven age. Products and services that we today take for granted—and which we are
incapable of creating on a household-by-household basis—were
unheard of in ancient times. We rely on a host of goods, services,
and infrastructure, unknown to the Ancients, to secure our families and create the conditions for physical survival and personal
development. Is communications equipment a necessity? Arguably as much as "wine" or "various types of flour." How would a
modern family fare without access to information services? Or to
reliable mechanized transportation? In the contemporary world,
these and other products and services determine prosperity and
sometimes life itself. They certainly reflect the concept of "necessities of life" articulated by the tradition.

What, on the other hand, are the "frankincense and costus
root" of our day that fall outside a Just Market profit constraint?
Among other things, they would almost certainly include vanity-

driven and luxury items; the Just Market would not likely expend resources policing the price of yachts.

The need to regularly revisit the meaning of access to life's basic necessities is as clear today as it was in the ancient period. As real incomes continue to fall for the majority, the cost of what are clearly basic necessities continues to rise. The cost of living in the US rose 12.1% in the five years since mid-2007. In the single year from June 2012 to June 2013, food costs increased by 2%; energy costs by 3.2%; shelter by 2.4%; transport by 2.5%; and medical by 3.1%. Meanwhile, real dollar minimum wages and subsidies dropped precipitously.[34] In Israel, increasingly high proportions of the population struggle; one-third of the work-force is employed part-time. Half of all new job openings, which are dominated by low-paying service opportunities, offer less than the official minimum wage.[35]

The modern policy debate over exactly which "necessities of life" should be included in price and profit regulations would be complex and ongoing. But the Just Market implies the need for that discussion when it calls for universal access to the products and services necessary to life today. And it identifies specific tools to ensure access to those requirements: price regulations, restrictions on commercial speculation, and a reasonable profit standard.

Price Regulation

In the third century, Just Market requirements for price regulation outraged segments of the Jewish merchant class (as they no doubt would today). Basing themselves on the commandment to "appoint magistrates and clerks for your tribes" (Deuteronomy 16:18), the Ancients called for market commissioners to assess the honesty and reasonability of daily transactions. When the policy was promulgated by Rabbi Judah Hanasi II (son of Rabbi Judah Hanasi, who is credited with the codification of the Oral Law), it was met with this hostile response:

> Those of the Nasi's House appointed market officers to oversee both measures and prices. Hearing that, Samuel said to Karna: "Go and teach them that market officers are appointed to oversee measures, but no such officers are appointed to oversee prices." But Karna delivered these words: "Market officers are appointed to oversee both measures and prices." The man said to him: "Is your name Karna? Let a horn grow out of your eye." And a horn did grow out of his eye. But whose opinion did Karna follow? ... (T)hat market officers are appointed to oversee both measures and prices, on account of the impostors.[36] (BT Bava Batra 89a)

Karna may have suffered his horn, but he continued to evangelize price regulation on behalf of Hanasi, promoting the anti-monopolist thread that runs through the Just Market. One thousand years later, Maimonides weighed in with this understanding of the Torah text:

> You shall appoint magistrates and officials ... (The meaning is that) they stand before the judges; they make their rounds to the markets, squares, and shops, fixing prices, regulating weights, and correcting abuses ... The courts are obligated to fix

market prices and put officers in charge of them.
(Maimonides, *Laws of Sale*, 14:2)

These commissioners ("magistrates") were tasked with
several responsibilities. They were roaming observers. They
inspected and regulated those all-important weights and
measures. They enforced honest transactions in the market.
And quite directly, they were to engage in "fixing prices." Their
reasoning mirrored that of modern economists such as Robert
Pollin, who suggest that "throughout the history of capitalism,
unregulated financial markets have persistently produced instability and crises."[37]

Worried by sharp price fluctuations, the Ancients tasked
the market commissioners with regulating prices in the interest
of stability. In addition to fending off price spikes among "things
which are life's necessities," they also applied constraints on rapid
price reductions, which they likewise viewed with alarm:

Our Rabbis taught: Public prayers, even on the
Sabbath, are offered for goods (which have become
dangerously cheap). (BT Bava Batra 91a)

When prices fell sharply and incongruently with supply
levels, the Ancients suspected market manipulators who intended
to destroy competition through unfair advantage and who, when
the dust settled, would move to predatory pricing. That's why they
considered radically reduced prices as noxious as those that were
excessively high. In fact, the Ancients were so concerned with
protecting consumers from predatory pricing that they used the
case of a fugitive prisoner to emphasize that even a criminal in

dire straits could not be subjected to an overcharge, in this case the outrageous sum of a *denar* for a ferryboat ride.

> If a man running away from prison came to a ferry and said to the boatman, "Take a *denar* to ferry me across," he would still have to pay him not more than the value of his services. (BT Bava Kamma 116a)

Speculation and Hoarding

The disruptive nature of large-scale monopoly threatens traditional Jewish economic values of stability and widespread prosperity. And so the Ancients oppose both monopoly and the tools of its empowerment—hoarding, speculation, and predatory pricing. Saving personal produce for bad times is permitted, but hoarding basic market goods with commercial intent is outlawed.

> Rav said: Fruit and things which are life's necessities, for instance, wines, oils and the various kinds of flour, must not be hoarded. But spices, cumin and pepper may be. Prohibitions apply to one buying from the market; but for one who brings in for his own, it is permitted. (BT Bava Batra 90b)

Market goods are hoarded for two purposes. The first is a prelude to rapacious competition. The second is to drive prices to a level at which the price disconnects from the real value of the commodity or product; that is, from a price that realistically reflects the cost of the product plus a reasonable profit. When predatory pricing takes hold, market stability falters. The price of other goods becomes less assured. Consumers trying to satisfy basic needs suffer, along with small business owners who must suddenly contend with erratic flows of commodities and finished product.

There is a wide gulf between speculation and productive modern forms of investment, one that the precapitalist Talmudic experience could not have imagined. What the Ancients did discern, though, were the evils of speculation, hoarding, and usury, and the eagerness of their practitioners to manipulate markets:

> Concerning those who hoard fruit, lend money on usury, reduce the measures and raise prices, Torah says, "When will the new moon be gone, that we may sell grain? And the Sabbath, that we may set forth corn? Making the ephah small, and the shekel great, and falsifying the balances of deceit."[38] (BT Bava Batra 90b)

That understanding prompted the Ancients to restrict allowable market practices, reining in the ability of wholesale dealers to hoard—and so, to speculate.

> A cattle dealer may . . . buy and slaughter, or buy and keep for the market. He may, however, not retain the animal he bought last for thirty days. (BT Bava Kamma 80a)

A commercial hoarder speculates on his ability to control prices by controlling supply. The most detrimental speculative activity often focuses on commodities of the broadest, most sustained demand, which are also those likely to be included in the category of "the necessities of life." The Sages don't use the term "commodity," but references to foods and "the necessities of life" permeate their discussion of hoarding and speculation.

By its nature, a commodity is what it is. A grain of wheat cannot be meaningfully differentiated from another of the same type and grade. Significant value is not added—otherwise it would not be considered a commodity.

Likewise, the speculator's investment does not develop any new social capacity. In this sense, speculating on a commodity like wheat is entirely different than investing in a wheat farm itself, or in research that aims to increase wheat yields—or even developing the Cap'n Crunch of a new generation. Commodity speculation succeeds when there are shortages and famine. It fails when the market is stable and well supplied. This is the essence of wrong that the Ancients identified.

After the global recession that began in 2008, hundreds of thousands of stock portfolios lunged at a lifeline in commodity investment. Within three years, $350 billion had been invested in speculative commodity funds.[39] At the same time, domestic food prices lurched upward, taxing the middle and lower classes in the US and sparking food riots around the globe.[40] The spike in food prices resulted from a series of economic, environmental, and technological factors, but only those speculating on food commodities benefited from the misery that developed from the shortages that were created around the world.

Gretchen Morgenson of the *New York Times* has noted that the majority of academic studies on this issue "demonstrate the ill effects of speculation on energy and food prices" internationally.[41] And Michel Barnier, the former European Commissioner for the Internal Market has commented that "speculation in basic foodstuffs is a scandal when there are a billion starving people in the world."[42] In addition to speculation in hard product commodities—an investment strategy that by its nature creates insecurity for millions, if not billions—commoditized financial derivatives, like the mass mortgage portfolios that helped trigger the worldwide financial crisis in 2008, also fall into the category of speculative commodity activity.

Commodity trading is generally accepted as an ethical form of investment in the Western world. The Ancients, on the other hand, condemned speculation, which succeeds by depriving people of the basis of survival. The Just Market advocates against speculative commodity funds and financial derivatives that serve no productive purpose, supporting legislation that limits or prohibits their fields of operation.

A Reasonable Profit Standard

The Sage Samuel, who adamantly opposed price regulation, nevertheless acknowledged the need to limit profit margins in the popular interest:

> Samuel said . . . that one may not profit more than one sixth. (BT Bava Metzia 40b) . . . And any profits on sales must not exceed one sixth. (BT Bava Batra 90a)

From the oral tradition of Mishnah through Talmudic discussion, to Maimonides and almost five hundred years later in the *Shulkhan Arukh*, the principle of a profit ceiling is repeated and codified:

> (E)ach merchant should not make all the profit he
> desires; indeed, the courts of law should fix a sixth
> as his profit and the seller should thus not profit
> more than a sixth. (Maimonides, *Laws of Sale* 14:1)

The Ancients repeatedly refer to a one-sixth standard regarding profit margins, overcharging, measurement, and even compensation of estate trustees.

One-sixth profit is the same as one-seventh of the total sale price.[43] Thus, the one-sixth standard may stem from the tradition's mystical use of the number seven (reflected in the seven-day cycle of creation; the weekly Sabbath; the Sabbatical Year; the seven circles around the walls of Jericho; etc.) or it may simply relate to the base-60 Babylonian numerical system. A contemporary yardstick of reasonable profit might be different. It is the need for a standard, not any specific permissible level, that lies at the core of the Just Market value.

Some economically conservative Orthodox commentators argue that even if a product is a "necessity of life" and so falls within the scope of profit regulation, the constraint applies only to broker-wholesalers, not to retail merchants, craft production, or services. But in the mid-sixteenth century, Yosef Caro's seminal Jewish legal reference, the *Shulkhan Arukh*, focused not on whether, but how a constraint should be applied to address different economic circumstances. Caro clearly extends the profit constraint beyond the wholesale sector, speaking directly to the situation of shopkeepers (merchants and craftsmen-producers) as distinct from broker-dealers.

> When does this (profit constraint) apply? When
> one sells all his merchandise together with no
> additional labor.[44] But a shopkeeper who sells his
> merchandise a little at a time—we estimate his
> labor and his expenses and he is permitted a profit
> of one sixth on them as well. (*Shulkhan Arukh*,
> Hoshen Mishpat 231:20)

Thus the *Shulkhan Arukh* argues that the profit constraint
applies equally to the wholesaler (the broker who invests "no additional labor") and the shopkeeper (who was also often the producer
of his wares). It suggests that in the case of wholesalers, the profit
constraint is calculated on the cost of the product alone. But if
a merchant invests his time in a shop—preparing the product,
fixing up the store, promoting his goods, or simply waiting for
customers—a reasonable profit standard would be calculated on
the cost of the product plus the shopkeeper's expenses and labor.

The notion of narrowing the profit constraint to wholesalers of basic foods is criticized by Meir Tamari, a widely
respected Orthodox writer on Jewish business ethics (more on
Tamari's work in appendix A). Tamari suggests that the historically accepted meaning of Talmudic passages like this one extend
to commodities in general and prohibit multiple profit centers for
similarly low value-added products.[45]

> Hoarders of fruit must not hoard, carry out, profit,
> twice in eggs. Prayers are offered and not caused
> to go out. (BT Bava Batra 90a) . . . Our Rabbis

taught: It is not permitted to make a profit in eggs twice. Mari ben Mari said: Rav and Samuel are in dispute. One says: Two for one. And the other says: By a dealer to a dealer. (BT Bava Batra 91a)

Here's what's constant between these contrasting views and other sources of the tradition: The "necessities of life"—however defined—should not be subject to profits beyond the regulated level or to multiple profit centers. As the Talmudic argument makes clear, there are two purposes. The first is to deter profiteering in necessities at the expense of the consuming public. The second is to maintain prices that put within arm's reach that same basket of necessary products.

The concept of a profit constraint is part of the Judaic ethic, despite historical pressure to belittle or ignore it. That pressure intensified with the development of capitalism and the capitalist ethos. As Eliezer Diamond, professor of Talmud at the Jewish Theological Seminary, notes, "In the medieval and the modern periods, Jewish law caved to the marketplace on this."[46]

Yet prominent contemporary economists, without apparent Talmudic influence, advocate for restraint on profits in the public interest. Economics journalist Robert Kuttner points to the World War II-era Renegotiation Board as a prime example of profit regulation that worked—and worked well—to constrain profit for the sake of the general welfare. In 2005, Kuttner proposed "an excess profits tax on the oil companies, who are reaping the benefits of tight oil supplies."[47] Nobel Laureate Joseph Stiglitz comments that "excess profits" in the financial sector (which he defines as "returns in excess of the normal return on capital") provide convincing evidence that "it is inconceivable that markets are really competitive."[48]

Excess Profit—The *Onah Portion*

The Ancients identified excess profit as the *Onah Portion*, defined as any balance remaining after expenses plus a 16.7% margin on them (equivalent to 14.3% of revenue). Permissible profit was calculated on the basis of total expenses rather than the sales used in accounting procedures today. Consequently, allowable profit distributions increase with the overall proportion of expenses to revenue—a tension between efficiency and values, but by no means one that is catastrophic for the modern capitalist.

A modern Onah calculation would be made on a firm-by-firm basis as the sum of annual costs and sales rather than transaction by transaction. Any firm in any "necessary" industry with profit levels above 16.7% on expenses would be assessed for an Onah Portion. The broad statistical record suggests a particular Onah propensity among firms in the mining, finance, insurance, and real estate sectors, and among holding companies. An Onah Portion would be less likely in most business segments with high operating cost percentages, such as manufacturing and retail industries. (The very profitable metal ore mining industry would be an exception due to the highly speculative treatment of many of its products. So are specific manufacturing segments, such as medical devices and software, that benefit from low capital costs and patent-protected products which are also candidates for a category of modern necessities.)

Because a modern profit constraint would be determined on a firm-by-firm basis, public information is not available that would allow us to determine exactly how much of the economy might be considered "excess profit." However, IRS statistics, which at the time of this writing are available through 2010, indicate that by applying the Onah definition to industry-wide data, excess profits in the US far exceed half a trillion dollars in some years.

In the latest four-year time series for which IRS data is available (2007–2010), excess corporate profit has not dipped below $370 billion in any one year, and has ranged as high as $570 billion in 2007. The four-year data understates the real figures for several reasons: First, calculations are based on corporate returns only; partnerships and limited liability corporations, which are especially prevalent in highly profitable sectors like real estate, are excluded from the calculations. Second, high-profit industry segments are not broken out in publicly available IRS tables, obscuring their Onah profits with broader industry totals. And finally, some individual firms in every industry perform far under Onah profit levels, so that the percentages of those firms that do surpass the "excess" profit level generate higher returns than are reported on an aggregate industry-wide basis.

Table 1-1. Selected Onah Portion Excess Profits 2007—2010 ($billion)

	2007	2008	2009	2010	4-Year Total
Metal Ore Mining	10.1	5.3	6.0	12.3	33.8
Tobacco Manufacturing	11.4	7.9	1.7	1.2	22.3
Software Publishers	7.7	3.9	6.0	8.3	25.9
Activities Related to Credit Intermediation	2.8	0.2	2.0	3.9	8.8
Commodity Contracts-Dealing-Brokerage	0.3	8.2	0.3	0.1	8.8
Securities-Commodity Exchanges	9.9	1.1	7.4	12.0	30.4
Funds-Trusts-Other Financial Vehicles	441.4	11.5	237.6	247.3	937.8
Lessors-Buildings	16.6	12.3	8.9	29.1	67.0
Lessors-Miniwarehouses	25.8	1.0	7.1	4.9	38.8
Lessors-Nonfinancial Intangible Assets	0.7	0.7	1.3	1.3	4.0
Scientific Research-Development	0.0	1.9	2.3	2.7	6.9
Offices of Other Holding Companies	15.6	20.0	21.7	30.8	88.2

IRS Corporation Source Book (excess profit calculations based on 16.7% maximum; additional industry detail for industries with excess profit is available in Appendix C.)

Between 2007 and 2010, IRS corporate data indicates that thirty-nine industry segments reported Onah-level profits. Of these, twelve reached excess profit levels in each of the four years (table 1-1). These twelve segments account for more than 70% of the total identifiable excess profits of more than $1.7 trillion over the period.

In the modern economy, the absence of any profit control mechanism strongly favors firms with relatively low operating costs, creating unusually high profit levels in many firms of certain types—think finance sector or digitally based industries. The profit control mechanism significantly reduces that disparity among sectors by linking maximum profits to expenditure levels, benefitting both the company and the common weal.

Under a Just Market concept, the Onah Portion of profit above 16.7% is *potentially* subject to surrender. In a modern application, what would have been considered excess profit subject to surrender might instead be retained by a company if it is applied to categories that speak to the needs of wage equity, employment expansion, and market stability—investments that increase common access to the necessities of life. *In a Just Market scenario, those choices, in turn, broaden the expense base and therefore increase distributable profit as owner or employee bonus compensation.* Here's how:

The specifics of an acceptable allocation of the Onah Portion are a matter of tax policy that would be determined from a broad social needs perspective. For example, perhaps a minimum of one-sixth would be allocated to increasing the wages of current employees, or to hiring additional staff. Another sixth could be put toward marketing and another to product development. One more sixth might be allocated to non-distributable retained earnings to build the long-term value of the firm and so enhance the stability of everyone involved in the company's life. Another sixth might be allocated to capital expenditures.

Qualified allocations taken to avoid Onah tax that are not expensed (a contribution to retained earnings, for example) would not be considered when calculating additional levels of expense for profit-taking purposes. Otherwise, the final sixth of the Onah Portion would then be available for additional owner distribution.

Because the level of distributable profit is based on total expenses, decisions to increase the number of employees, raise average compensation rates, reduce income gaps, and reinvest in the company all create the opportunity to proportionately increase owners' compensation. As the company's contribution toward the social value of full and equitable employment increases, so do its owners' profit opportunities.

Primarily as a means of sorting between wage compensation and regulated profit, the Just Market structure might establish a *Wage Equity Parameter* that is consistent with the general Talmudic standard of equity; that is, that no individual wage and benefit package can total more than six times the corresponding package paid to any other employee.[49] (With initial support from the centrist Kadima Party, which was then in power, a similarly structured but weaker and unsuccessful Wage Gap Reduction Bill was introduced in the Israeli Knesset in 2007. A stronger measure was more recently defeated in a Swiss referendum.)[50]

The Wage Equity Parameter yardstick *does not limit total owner compensation* to that standard; it merely regulates *wage* gaps. As an accounting tool, this method differentiates true net profit and earned wages from a potential Onah Portion. Additional compensation may be distributed through various forms of profit sharing (direct, stock, or ownership). *In conjunction with the regu-*

lated profit maximum, wage gap parameters create a significant incentive for business owners to increase employment and income equity.

The mechanism that allows for wage compensation plus the one-sixth profit for owner-operators was clarified in the passage cited earlier from the *Shulkhan Arukh*. Owners who spend their time in daily operations are clearly entitled to a salary that is included as an "expense" for the determination of maximum profit distribution. It's obvious that if an owner-operator did not perform the work, someone else would be paid to do it. The owner-operator's salary compensation is therefore a valid part of the expense of maintaining the business, as long as the salary package itself falls within the wage gap parameters (not more than six times average) of the Just Market structure.

Larger firms that reach the Onah Portion threshold are generally in a position to accommodate Onah Portion requirements. More relaxed standards will be required for smaller firms, and especially those in which owner-operators constitute an important part of the workforce. One possibility would be to exclude a fixed amount of profit—say $500,000—from owner compensation and profit in the calculation of the Onah Portion, providing a buffer for small business owner-operators from real hardship resulting from the Onah requirements.

The argument against the profit constraint is, of course, that high profits drive economic growth, reinvestment, and prosperity. But that's not the case. During the years 2002-2010, median US household income went up by 16%.[51] But during the same period, net corporate income increased by 74%—almost five times as much.[52] And in Israel's highly touted economy, more than half of the country's population remains at risk for poverty; 21% live below the line, while another 31% are on the precipice.[53]

Nobel Economics Prize winner Paul Krugman wonders, despite the prevalence of high profits and low borrowing costs,

> . . . why aren't we seeing a boom in business invest-
> ment? Well, there's no puzzle here if rising profits
> reflect rents (profits that don't represent returns on
> investment but instead reflect the value of market
> dominance), not returns on investment. A monop-
> olist can, after all, be highly profitable yet see no
> good reason to expand its productive capacity.[54]

Is it true, on the other hand, that a constraint on maximum profit will deaden an economy? If I were told by an investor that he "only" achieved a one-sixth return per year, that wouldn't seem too shabby, in our current environment or any other. And reserve funds have been mandated for financial and insurance companies for decades; experience has proven their wisdom. Why would incentivized expenditures to various socially responsive categories that build long-term stability and reasonable income equity be any less socially useful—or less ethical?

From Ethics to Advocacy

Left to its own devices, a competitive economy produces inequalities; both Just Market and Western capitalist paradigms recognize that. But how much inequality is too much? The rapidly growing disparity between the availability of goods and services conducive to productive civic life and the affordability of those same goods and services suggests the scale of a problem that calls out for remedy. In the current economic environment, the rising cost of living is rooted in excessive pricing and profits—even as real income of the wage-earning population decreases, minimum-wage workers lose ground, and the subsidized poor trail further behind. As a result, we are enmeshed in a no-win predicament that complicates, rather than promotes, access to the necessities of life for an increasing proportion of the population.

The Just Market is not content with a welfare-based safety net that variously feeds the poor, offers subsidies to those in dire need, and reluctantly creates jobs programs that may or may not result in consistent employment. Instead, its objective is to provide universal and ongoing access to the necessities of life through productive means.

The Just Market referees the competitive arena to assure that the mechanics of competition facilitate rather than obstruct access to the necessities of life. This central Just Market requirement is reflected in four policies:

- *Conduct an ongoing review of "the necessities of life"* to assure that regulations accurately describe individual and family requirements to function successfully in the current social, personal, and economic environment.

- *Institute price regulations that cover the necessities of life*, promoting universal access to them.

- *Outlaw harmful speculative financial instruments*, including commodity speculation and financial hedges and derivatives that are not based on underlying asset values.

- *Establish a maximum profit standard* (16.7% of expense or 14.3% of revenue is suggested by Talmudic commentators) that invites competition and innovation but promotes the availability of necessities to the population; and *enforce an excess profits (Onah) tax* whose proceeds are devoted to the development of jobs. Any company can reduce or avoid the Onah tax and elevate allowable profit levels by reinvesting in more equitable wages, additional employment, and other socially useful measures that are determined by policy guidelines.

2. UNIVERSAL EMPLOYMENT OPPORTUNITY

The Book of Ruth opens a detailed window on the ancient work environment, including the practice of gleaning. In the process, Ruth provides a critical link to Just Market support of full employment policies in the modern world.

Ruth, Torah, and Mishnah Pe'ah, a tractate of the original Oral Law, together establish the value of universal employment opportunity through four instruments: the obligation of farmers to set aside fields for the poor and dispossessed; the right of those same populations to enter private fields and glean the crops; the establishment of gleanings as "property" of the poor, poetically iterated as "the alien, the fatherless and widow"; and the definition of any obstruction of their rights to glean as "robbery."

The Gleaning Concept

There are no commandments in the Book of Ruth, no laws. The story is simple. A non-Jewish woman accompanies her mother-in-law, Naomi, on her return to Judea after her son—Ruth's husband—dies. Despite Naomi's roots in Judea, she has been gone for many years and is without means of support.

The women arrive in Judea at the time of the barley harvest. Ruth enters the fields to glean for grain left behind by the reapers. She encounters Boaz, the owner of the field, who is also a distant relative of Naomi. Naomi later counsels Ruth to spruce up and go to Boaz at night. Ruth does, asking Boaz to "lay his cloak" over her.

Those familiar with the story usually identify two values with the Book of Ruth: personal loyalty and fair, gracious behavior toward "strangers" living in Jewish communities.[55] Ruth demonstrates her allegiance by accompanying Naomi to an unfamiliar land to live among an unfamiliar people. She shares with Naomi the small portion of grain she gleans from the fields. Ruth is ultimately rewarded for her loyalty and faith by becoming the great-grandmother of the shepherd who grows to be David, King of Judea.

The time that Ruth spent gleaning is often overlooked in favor of the personal loyalty theme of the story. But when the text is examined from the perspective of employment policy and workplace ethics, what emerges is a set of social behaviors that directly reflect the thinking of the Ancients from Torah through Talmud and into the medieval Jewish world. Those values remain arguably relevant in the economic turmoil of modern times:

> When you reap the harvest of your land, you shall not reap all the way to the edges of your field, or gather the gleanings of your harvest. You shall not pick your vineyard bare, or gather the fallen fruit of your vineyard; you shall leave them for the poor

and the stranger. (Leviticus 19: 9–10, substantially repeated at Leviticus 23:22)

The text identifies three types of gleaning through three negative commandments. Do not reap the corners of the field (*pe'ah* or corner). Do not gather what is left behind when the fields are harvested (*leket* or "collection"). Do not pluck every grape in the vineyard nor pick up what drops (*shikhekhah* or "forgotten"). Ruth works at the most demanding type of gleaning, the leket. She competes for produce dropped or overlooked by paid reapers in the fields. This category is the most widely recognized of the three forms of gleaning, made familiar by the French artist Jean Francois Millet's image of peasant women hunched over leavings in a picked-over field.

Millet may have painted an accurate picture of gleaning as it was practiced in Christian Europe, where it was commonly proffered as charity to the despised poor. But gleaning—and gleaners—were understood somewhat differently in ancient Jewish society.

For more than a thousand years, Jewish communities protected gleaning as a recognized right of the poor and an obligation of landowners. Excerpts from Torah, the Talmud, and the Book of Ruth graphically describe the responsibilities, the rights, and the process involved. Landowners' gleaning obligations were restated in Deuteronomy, probably several hundred years after Leviticus was written:

> When you reap the harvest in your field and over-
> look a sheaf, do not turn back to get it; it shall go
> to the stranger, the fatherless, and the widow . . .

> When you shake the fruit from your olive trees,
> do not go over them again; that shall go to the
> stranger, the fatherless, and the widow. When you
> gather the grapes of your vineyard, do not pick it
> over again; that shall go to the stranger, the father-
> less, and the widow. (Deuteronomy 24: 19–21)

Deuteronomy seems to have surfaced in an era of spiritual revival spurred by the reformist Judean King Hezekiah. Its text restates the law in the affirmative, providing instructions for each category of gleaning, then repeating an identical list of beneficiaries for emphasis: the stranger, the fatherless, and the widow.

Whether discussing the leket, pe'ah, or shikhekhah, the Ancients consistently crafted the law to err in favor of the poor—and to deal harshly with landowners who did not comply:

> If grain was heaped and leket from it had not
> yet been collected, even if (the owner) piled the
> wheat in an area that had grown oats, a fine was
> imposed. Whatever touches the ground belongs to
> the poor. If the wind scattered the crop, estimate
> the amount of leket the field would have normally
> yielded; give that to the poor. Rav Shimon ben
> Gamliel says: "Do not estimate; Instead, give to
> the poor the usual amount that falls (as leket)."
> (Mishnah Pe'ah 5:1)

> Rav Meir says, "That which is doubtful is still a
> gleaning." (Mishnah Pe'ah 4:11) ... What is meant
> by the statement (in which Torah says: "You must

not pick the small clusters from your vineyard")
". . . any cluster (of grapes) which has neither a
shoulder nor drippings? If the grapes hang down,
it belongs to the owner; if there is doubt, it belongs
to the poor." (Mishnah Pe'ah 7:4)

This, then, is the backdrop to Ruth's entry into the fields.
Even in the unlikely event that she comprehended an oral law
that would not be codified for another thousand years, we can
imagine Ruth's confusion as she steps tentatively into the broad,
cacophonous field filled with sweat, curses, the whir of scythes,
and the blurred motion of hands snatching cut stalks as they fall.
Employed reapers precede the gleaners through the fields. They
are paid a wage but may also be compensated with a portion of
their pickings, which they guard jealously.

The gleaners jostle for the leavings with enough spirit that
the concerned Sages issue a warning to protect the weaker among
them:

They (the gleaners) may not reap with scythes or
spades, lest they strike at one another. (Mishnah
Pe'ah 4:4)

The scene must have been a puzzle to Ruth. It also likely
terrified her. She is almost visibly relieved when Boaz, the owner
of the field, approaches to offer advice and some aid:

Stay here close to my (reaper) girls. Keep your eyes
on the field they are reaping and follow them. I have
ordered the men not to molest you. (Ruth 2:2–9)

But why would Boaz counsel Ruth to stay close to the reapers, who may, after all, have it in for a woman, a foreigner, and a newcomer to the fields? The Mishnah illuminates the scene:

> What constitutes leket? That which falls while reaping is in progress. If a man was reaping, and grasped a handful of the crop, but a thorn pricked him so that what he held fell to the ground, it is still the owner's. That which is inside the reaper's hand and then drops, or inside the sickle, belongs to the poor. But what drops behind the hand or outside the sickle is to the owner. Rav Yishma'el says: "That which falls from the top of the hand or the top of the sickle[56] belongs to the poor." But Rav Akiva says: "It belongs to the owner." (Mishnah Pe'ah 4:10)

Whether Rav Yishma'el or Rav Akiva prevailed, one thing is certain: gleaners had to react quickly as the leket fell from the hand of a reaper before them. Did the grain drop from "inside the hand" or from the outside? Did it fall as the result of a thorn prick or from clumsiness due to the hurried pace of the reaping? If Ruth couldn't discern the facts quickly, she might trigger an argument with a reaper reclaiming his grain. If she hesitated because she had not clearly seen how the stalk had dropped, another gleaner would snatch it before she decided. Without a doubt, leket gleaners worked so closely behind paid reapers that the cause for each stalk of fallen barley could be witnessed, judged, and acted upon in rapid succession.

The Right to Gainful Employment Opportunity

The Ancients understood the connection between gainful employment and life. The imperative to save a life extended into the realm of labor, where denying a worker his wages was linked to the denial of life (Deuteronomy 24:15). The Talmud, too, links the limited ability of a person to find gainful employment to the desperate measures he is willing to take to obtain and protect it:

> Why does (the worker) climb a ladder or hang from a tree or risk death? . . . "His life depends on (his wages)" indicates that anyone who denies a hired laborer his wages, it is as though he takes his life from him. (BT Bava Metzia 112a)

Millet's forlorn peasants would not have been recognizable as gleaners in Jewish society, because there, gleaning was *a matter of right* for the needy and dispossessed. As the Mishnah examines the gleaning categories in turn, in each case the Sages determine that obstructing the process, or withholding the opportunity to glean from the poor, is out-and-out robbery. And if withholding wages "is as though he takes his life from him," then the denial of employment opportunity that by right belongs to the laborer is surely no less grievous. According to the Ancients, it is, in fact, outright stealing: "One who prevents the poor from gathering . . . is a robber of the poor" (Mishnah Pe'ah 5:6).

One may be robbed of an opportunity to work in the gleaning fields, as the Sages indicate here. But they also assert that not only is the opportunity to labor a right, so is the compensation, here in the form of produce, which would be earned. Rav Meir terms it "the property of the poor":

> Rav Meir says: "He (the landowner) may thin his own (portion), but not that part *which is the property of the poor.*" (Mishnah Pe'ah 7:5; italics added)

Two different rights accrued, then, to the poor and to those oppressed classes disproportionately represented in their ranks: the stranger, the orphan, and the widow. First, the opportunity right to glean, and second, the property right to the portion that would be gathered during the gleaning season. Together with the mandatory obligation of landowners to provide and oversee the gleaning process, the guarantee of gainful labor opportunity was sealed. This social contract forms the mechanism to assure access to the necessities of life for the most needy members of society. As economist Robert Pollin remarks, "Without full employment, the fundamental notion of equal rights for everyone . . . faces insurmountable obstacles in practical implementation."[57]

The Business Obligation

Torah does not specify a precise proportion of fields or amount of product to set aside for gleanings. But, in an example of a critical gap in the source text that was later satisfied by the Oral Law, the Mishnah established a standard that provided modest flexibility for larger and smaller farmers:

> One should not make the pe'ah less than one-sixtieth of the entire crop. And though there no definite amount is given for pe'ah, it is all based upon the size of the field, the number of poor who will be collecting it, and the abundance of the crop. (Mishnah Pe'ah 1:2)

The pe'ah gleaning category required that all produce in the corner of each field be left for gleaners *in addition* to the leket requirement for general collection of left-behind crops (Mishnah Pe'ah 1:2). All crops, orchards, and vineyards within the set-aside area belonged to the gleaners. Landowners were required to designate pe'ah sections for each crop, each variety of crop, and each quality of produce.

Precise delineation of the pe'ah section was required at the start of each planting season, thwarting the temptation for landowners to scout for low-yield sections just before harvest, then designating those for the pe'ah portion at the last moment.

Rav Shimon offers four reasons for this requirement. First, as a precaution against robbing the poor of the most bountiful portions of the field. Second, as protection against wasting the time of the poor while they waited for the landowner's selection. Third, as a shield for the conscientious landowner who might otherwise be falsely accused of ignoring the pe'ah if his designation were delayed. Finally, Rav Shimon suggests that permitting a delay could entice owners to claim that they had already designated a pe'ah set-aside when, in fact, they had not. Rabba gets to the same point later in the same Talmudic folio, albeit more succinctly: "It is a precaution against cheats" (BT Shabbat 23a–b).

Landowners were forbidden to withhold any field, any type or quality of produce from the gleaners. Pe'ah could be designated as a section of standing crop, as harvested sheaves, or as grain on the threshing floor at the end of the field (BT Bava Kamma 94a). Whichever the case, if a farmer grew two different crops or grains, a pe'ah set-aside was required for each:

If a man sows with two types of seed, even if he
only threshes both together, he must give pe'ah
twice. If a man sows a single field with two species
of wheat and threshes together, he gives pe'ah only
once, but if separately, then he creates two pe'ah
portions. (Mishnah Pe'ah 2:5)

If a portion of a crop had been harvested as fresh produce,
and a portion left to dry for longer-term storage, then a pe'ah
portion was required for each type in order to assure the poor of
the equitable value of their property share:

One who plucks fresh onions for the market and
leaves others in the ground to dry and store later
must give pe'ah from each separately. The same
applies to beans and to a vineyard.[58] (Mishnah
Pe'ah 3:3)

There was some—but not much—room for deviation be-
low the standard, even if a farmer's harvest went sadly awry. A total
disaster was required for a landowner to avoid pe'ah altogether:

If a field was harvested by . . . robbers, or if ants
chewed it up or locusts consumed it; or if it was
broken by wind or an animal, then the owner is
exempt (from providing pe'ah) . . . But if robbers
harvested half, and the owner harvested half,
then he gives a corner from what he harvested.
If he harvested half, and sells it, and takes half for
himself, he gives a corner for all of it. (Mishnah
Pe'ah 3:7–8)

Like the pe'ah and the leket, shikhekhah (forgotten fruit) obligations were required over and above those of the other forms of gleaning. The shikhekhah is similar to the leket in that it deals with the remnant from the harvest—in this case from vineyards and orchards, primarily olives and grapes:

> What is meant by the statement (in which the Torah says: "You must not pick the small clusters from your vineyard")? Any cluster which has neither a shoulder nor drippings. If it has a shoulder or the grapes hang down, it belongs to the owner; if there is doubt, it belongs to the poor. If there is a small cluster on the joint of a vine, and it can be nipped off with the cluster, it belongs to the owner. If not, it belongs to the poor. (Mishnah Pe'ah 7:4)

This description is reminiscent of the Ancients' painstaking assessment of the conditions that qualified grain that falls from the hand of a reaper as leket. Likewise parallel is their insistence that olives or grapes that qualify for shikhekhah are not charity, but rather the legal property of the poor (cited earlier at Mishnah Pe'ah 7:5).

The owners of olive orchards were permitted to shake the trees and go through the vineyards only once before turning them over to the poor. They were obligated to monitor their fields to assure that the intended recipients benefited from the law. The general population was barred from gleaning the fields, vineyards, and olive groves until "after the last of the poor" had gone through and taken what they needed; until after the poor had gleaned the

vineyards not once, but twice; and after two rainfalls had brought
down virtually all of the olives that were likely to fall from the
trees of their own accord.[59]

> At what point in time are all (not just the poor)
> permitted to take the leket? After the last of the
> poor had gone. And in the case of fallen grapes and
> small clusters of them, when are they permitted
> to anyone (not just the poor)? After the poor had
> gone through the vineyard and returned again.
> And in the case of olive trees? After the second
> rainfall. Rav Yehuda said, "And what if one has
> not harvested his olive trees until after the second
> rain has come? In that case, when the poor go out,
> and they have not brought back even four *issar*."[60]
> (Mishnah Pe'ah 8:1)

In sum, landowners had a legal responsibility to provide
gleaning opportunity to the poor on a regular basis, and in three
distinct forms. While we do not know what the total percentage
of the three categories allotted to gleaners might have been, we do
know that the accepted standard for the pe'ah category alone was
1.67% of the field, with the benefit of the leket and shikhekhah
added to it.

The Responsibility to Work

The gleaning laws presented the poor with a social contract. Each
indigent person was *guaranteed the opportunity to labor* and claim
her right to glean at each harvest. That contract offer was perma-

nent. While no one was forced to glean, labor was required at each harvest as a prerequisite to any individual's claim to gleanings. The opportunity right was an entitlement, but the fruit of the property right had to be earned. Gleaning was brutal work, no doubt about it. But it was also the kernel of a three-thousand-year-old Jewish policy supporting full employment.

Gleaning aside, charitable community funds were maintained to help the poor who needed assistance (BT Bava Batra 8a-b). But those who chose not to labor in the guaranteed gleaning job surrendered their share of the class-based property claim that Torah had invested in them. In the eyes of Jewish society, the physically capable diminished their own dignity by choosing to remain passive recipients of charity when opportunities for productive labor were present. The Ancients placed value on labor that promoted self-worth. Those who despised the value of even nasty, menial work like skinning and tanning were cautioned:

> Rav said to Rav Kahana: Deal in carcasses, but do not deal in words, flay carcasses in the market place and earn wages and do not say, "I am a priest and a great man and it is beneath my dignity." (Pesakhim 113a)

Of course, gleaning was only an option during the three ancient harvest seasons. No one could survive year-round by gleaning alone. The destitute relied on day labor and the community chest to see them through the rest of the year.

But the law stipulated the full employment contract to the extent that the ancient agrarian economy could support it. Even modest landowners were obligated to establish a gleaning corner despite the financial hardship posed by the law. To defray the burden, landowners were permitted to deduct the value of gleanings from religious tithes.

The confluence of the right to work and the responsibility to labor is emblematic of the traditional Jewish view of *tzedakah*.[61] Maimonides has this to say about the highest form of assistance to the poor in his formulation on the subject, the eight-step ladder of tzedakah:

> The highest degree (of helping the poor), exceeded by none, is that of a person who assists a poor Jew by providing him with a gift or a loan or by accepting him into a business partnership or by helping him find employment—in a word, by putting him where he can dispense with other people's aid. (Maimonides, *Laws of Gifts to the Poor*, 10:7)

Almost one thousand years earlier, the practical effect of the gleaning laws had underscored the same point. The laws decreed the provision of productive work and a mechanism that made that work available to anyone who wanted it. Labor was the essential vehicle for securing the necessities of life.

The Ancients created meaningful incentives for every unemployed person to step up to the plate. They obligated employers to maintain standard set-asides for the unemployed. And they praised the value of labor so that the unemployed would be encouraged to seize available opportunities.

A Modern Pe'ah Set-Aside

The free market paradigm incorporates a socially acceptable level of involuntary unemployment, usually pegged at about 5%. During recessionary periods, such as those recently experienced in the US, the official unemployment rate, of course, climbs much higher.

Unemployment extends significantly beyond the official unemployment rate, defined as including only persons who are without any paid work and have actively sought work (beyond reading ads) within the most recent four weeks. This definition excludes part-time workers who cannot find full-time jobs, as well as "discouraged workers," a formally recognized class which wants to work but has given up the active pursuit after a period of longer than four weeks.

The growth of these three groups in the last full decade of measurement (which excludes a large but ambiguous fourth "marginal" group also tracked by Bureau of Labor Statistics data) has been breathtaking. Between 2002 and 2012, the total number of official unemployed, discouraged workers and forced part-time workers together climbed by more than 56% to over 20.4 million— an "expanded unemployment" rate of 13.2%. During the first half of 2013, official unemployment dropped by half a point—but the number of both economically forced part-time employment and of discouraged workers grew by double digits since the first of the year, leading to an increase in the more realistic "expanded" unemployment rate to 13.5%—over twenty-one million people.[62]

Beyond unemployment statistics, the long-term trend of a widening prosperity gap is well documented. Between 1979 and 2009, real income in the US increased 72.7% for the top 5% of US families, while the lowest 20% experienced a decrease of 7.4%.[63] Economists Thomas Piketty and Emmanuel Saez have shown that since 1977, more than 15% of US national income shifted from the bottom 90% of the population to the top 10%, with 60% of income growth going to the top 1%.[64] The impact of high unemployment levels within this context of increasing income inequality devastates not only disadvantaged individuals involved, but the economic structure of modern society. Robert Kuttner notes that

> In the late 1990s, when we had full employment, in one three-year period Social Security's Year of Reckoning was set back by eight years, from 2029 to 2037 . . . And if wages rose with productivity growth, as they did until the late 1970s, Social Security would enjoy a perpetual surplus and we could raise benefits.[65]

Even in periods of relative growth, industry-specific instability calls out for a remedy. Between 1982 and 1986, while I was still a welder, more than 26% of all US shipbuilders—about thirty thousand workers—lost their jobs. By 1996, another twenty-six thousand were gone.[66] Some of the early layoffs—not all—were covered by especially generous unemployment compensation only because the jobs had been lost to foreign firms. But that funding ran out. Former shipbuilders were never again able to apply the skills they had learned, even to sorely needed public works projects that would require many thousands of welders, metal fitters, riggers, and other skilled and semiskilled workers. In the absence of a universal employment opportunity policy, there was no employer-obligated jobs program that fed productive work. Instead, unemployment checks provided temporary relief—but not work or the pride that comes with it.

Bridging the gulf between society's wealth and the remoteness of that wealth from increasing numbers of people requires a publicly regulated employment program—similar in scope to those represented in the gleaning laws, but in keeping with modern economic capabilities. The private sector has demonstrated that, despite its enormous energy, it will not undertake such a task of its own volition.

A modern Pe'ah Set-Aside might be "gleaned" as a fixed portion of gross business expenses, as was the ancient pe'ah, to create employment opportunity. The pe'ah laws set aside one-sixtieth of the field; that is, the cost to the farmer equaled 1.67% of his expenses. A modern Pe'ah Set-Aside could be similarly pegged at one-sixtieth of total expenses of every company.[67] The full amount of the Pe'ah Set-Aside would be dedicated to funding new employment.

Like the ancient practice, a modern pe'ah would be most effectively organized and delivered on an employer-by-employer basis, where each firm would have the option of reinvesting up to 100% of its Pe'ah Set-Aside each year through the employment of additional workers. Those firms that chose not to invest in new jobs with their Pe'ah Set-Aside account would deposit their contribution to a publicly administered Pe'ah Fund. The Fund would, in turn, finance the labor costs of an ongoing public works program to employ the unemployed—the highest form of tzedakah—while undertaking desperately needed improvements to public infrastructure.

A Pe'ah Set-Aside benefit would have totaled more than $313 billion in 2010 (one-sixtieth of business receipts less reported net income). The Set-Aside would fund more than six million jobs at a cost of $50,000 per job, or more than four million jobs at $75,000—over two million of them in construction and manufacturing. Pre-recession figures for the Pe'ah Set-Aside are, of course, even larger.

IRS data (table 2-1) suggests that the average firm in most sectors could easily handle a pe'ah obligation, almost certainly more easily than did farmers in ancient Judea. Over 83% of the $1.8 trillion in reported US corporate profits (2010) would be retained. Figures for net business income are calculated after all current-level officer and executive salaries are paid, and even after paper deductions for amortization, depletion, and depreciation. Not a single US business sector would dip into the red by satisfying its Pe'ah Set-Aside obligation.

Table 2-1. 2010 Pe'ah Set-Aside and Job Creation Projections

	($Billion)			Jobs	
	Sales	Expenses	Set-Aside	@ 50k/yr	@ 75k/yr
Total	20,587	18,750	313	6,262,597	4,175,065
Agriculture	122	112	2	37,498	24,998
Mining	303	247	4	82,636	55,091
Utilities	361	346	6	115,638	77,092
Construction	775	729	12	243,400	162,267
Manufacturing	5,879	5,359	89	1,789,817	1,193,211
Wholesale Trade	3,212	3,086	52	1,030,651	687,101
Retail Trade	2,801	2,692	45	899,086	599,390
Transport-Warehousing	558	529	9	176,614	117,743
Information	808	707	12	236,256	157,504
Finance-Insurance	2,602	2,140	36	714,851	476,568
Real Estate Rental-Leasing	211	152	3	50,878	33,919
Professional Services	875	788	13	263,052	175,368
Management of Companies	604	510	9	170,263	113,509
Administrative-Support-Waste Mgt.	364	339	6	113,215	75,477
Educational Services	56	48	1	15,940	10,627
Health Care-Social Assistance	533	487	8	162,762	108,508
Arts-Entertainment-Recreation	52	45	1	15,120	10,080
Accommodation-Food Services	325	300	5	100,080	66,720
Other Services	144	134	2	44,832	29,888

(IRS Corporation Source Book 2010; Pe'ah Set-Aside calculated at 1.67% of Expenses)

Perhaps the closest US effort toward similar objectives was embodied in the Full Employment and Balanced Growth Act of 1978, more commonly known as the Humphrey-Hawkins Bill. In its own words, the bill's objectives were to:

> . . . translate into practical reality the right of all Americans who are able, willing, and seeking to work to full opportunity for useful paid employment at fair rates of compensation; to assert the responsibility of the Federal Government to use all practicable programs and policies to promote full employment, production, and real income, balanced growth, adequate productivity growth.

The Act encourages reliance on the private sector to carry out its objectives. If the private sector fails in that effort, then it is left to the public sector to generate public employment venues that do. In this regard, Humphrey-Hawkins mirrors—and as a matter of policy accommodates—the Pe'ah Set-Aside. The major difference is that Humphrey-Hawkins never created an enforceable mechanism to realize its goals. The Pe'ah Set-Aside mechanism ensures a reservoir of funds focused on full employment, embodying both the wisdom of the Ancients and contemporary visionaries such as Joseph Stiglitz, who asserts that "(We need) a fiscal policy to maintain full employment—with equality. The most important government policy influencing well-being, with the most important consequences for distribution, is maintaining full employment."[68]

Technology Benefits and Responsibility

In the Talmudic era, labor was most often episodic; day laborers and craftsmen for hire dominated the market. As a result, the Ancients never considered an employer's long-term responsibility for a fixed set of workers. In that sense, any obligation of a landowner for reductions in labor demand was not a consideration. While the *treatment* of employees of the moment was a real concern for the Ancients (chapter 5), employers had no obligation to retain specific workers on an extended basis when there was no need for their labor.

But the Ancients did indeed comment on the issue of labor demand in a little-noticed passage regarding the shikhekhah (forgotten fruit) form of gleaning.

First, they agree that "a single piece ... is a gleaning," meaning that a solitary grape that falls from the vine belongs to the poor (Mishnah Pe'ah 7:4). They go on to explain that a single grape that pops off the cluster as it is snipped by the landowner or his paid worker remains the property of the landowner—in contrast to one that falls from the vine with no human intervention:

> What is a single grape? One that fell in the season of the grape harvest. If one was harvesting grapes, and he was cutting clusters of grapes that were entangled in leaves, and they fell from his hand to the earth and they were made into single grapes, indeed, this belongs to the master of the house. (Mishnah Pe'ah 7:3)

Having established the landowner's rights, the Ancients note a striking exception:

If one leaves a basket under the vine in the season
that he harvests grapes, indeed, he is openly stealing from the poor.

It would have been impossible to discern whether the
grapes that found their way into the bucket fell naturally from
the tree (and therefore belonged to the gleaners) or whether they
were the result of "cutting clusters of grapes . . . (so that) they fell
from (the reaper's) hand to the earth and they were made into
single grapes." The text applies to shikhekhah fruit, of whatever
origin, that fell into the strategically placed harvest basket.

What is the nature of this basket? It is, quite simply, a
harvesting tool that requires neither human hands nor even pres-
ence to effectively conclude its work. By its very infallible nature,
the basket sits inert, catching the fallen grapes, claiming them for
the landowner rather than those who would take them with their
own labor. It is a primitive mechanism. And so, the basket itself
is forbidden, reserving the labor opportunity for the paid reapers
and gleaners.

The catch basket introduces a cost savings at the expense
of labor. It requires neither gleaners nor harvesters and, as the
Ancients perceived it, robbed both of labor opportunity. The
Ancients react to this basic threat to the well-being of the workforce by outlawing the basket. By applying the formula that
identifies employers who utilize the catch basket with those who
"openly steal from the poor," the Just Market assigns an obligation to maintain labor opportunity where corresponding mechanisms are introduced. In the age of technology, that concern is
more germane than ever before. Without protection, workers
whose jobs depend on the *absence* of a specific technology are left

without recourse. What remains in the worst situations is, simply, an incentive to get rid of them.

I saw this truth at a personal level: over the course of only a couple of years, industrial welding changed forever. Before, there was only "stick" welding: take one coated metal rod, twist it into a "stinger," burn it down, and reload. Suddenly, automatic welding guns dominated the work floor—endless spools of wire that flowed like warm butter and seared the eyes with a constant, harsh electric arc. Task quotas jumped by multiples of six, then ten. More production, more fatigue, more eye injuries—and far fewer welders. Older, infirm workers who had persevered through shipyard winters and stifling summers for decades were fired for "lack of production." They simply disappeared; technology trumped humanity.

In the US, productivity and hourly compensation rose more or less in tandem between 1947 and 1979 (188% and 100%, respectively). But over the next two decades, productivity continued a swift upward climb (80%) while compensation rose only one-tenth as much.[69] Since 1990, in better and worse times alike, labor productivity has increased significantly more rapidly than employment. The gap between productivity and employment has accelerated during the most concentrated periods of upward wealth concentration—in the years 2000–2011, for example (table 2-2).

Table 2-2. Productivity and Employment Change

	Change	
	Productivity	Employment
1990—2000	25.7%	16.4%
2000—2007	21.8%	6.3%
2007—2011	9.3%	-3.7%

US Bureau of Labor Statistics

Free market common wisdom holds that—by definition—productivity improvements benefit everyone. But Erik Brynjolfsson of MIT concludes that "Productivity can go up and the economic pie gets bigger, but the majority of people don't share in that gain."[70] And even conservative commentators concede that advancing technology will continue to be a more dominant cause of unemployment than trade policy or other factors.[71]

As in the time of the Ancients, the mechanics of productivity often penalize the average employee in the workforce. And, as in ancient times, protections are needed. A *Shikhekhah Labor Displacement Fund* would allocate a portion of technology-based savings from annual productivity improvements—say, half—to those who are placed at risk by them. To assess the Shikhekhah Fund obligation, each firm would measure its productivity change on an annual basis, then apply a fixed percentage of each year's improvement to the Set-Aside in the following year. Shikhekhah Fund proceeds would be allocated to retraining, job relocation, and new venture funding channeled specifically to employees dislocated by productivity advances. The Fund would be administered much like state-level unemployment compensation funds; companies contribute to and pull from individually tracked accounts that, if overdrawn, trigger a requirement for additional contributions.

The Shikhekhah Labor Displacement Fund is not a punishment for technology. It allocates newly available dollars, a portion of the benefit of productivity improvements, to directly aid those employees who suffer loss as a result of new technologies. It is a remedy to the conundrum recognized by Paul Krugman, who asks whether

. . . innovation and progress (can) really hurt large numbers of workers, maybe even workers in general?. . . (T)he truth is that it can, and serious economists have been aware of this possibility for almost two centuries.[72]

Training and Mentoring

So what about Ruth? When we last saw her, she was entering the busy field to find barley overlooked by the reapers:

> Ruth came and gleaned in a field, behind the reapers … Boaz said to the servant who was in charge of the reapers, "Whose girl is that?" The servant replied, "She is a Moabite girl who came back with Naomi from the country of Moab.". . . Boaz said to Ruth, "Stay here close to my girls. Keep your eyes on the field they are reaping and follow them. I have ordered the men not to molest you. And when you are thirsty, go to the jars and drink some water." (Ruth 2:2–9)

Jewish tradition praises Boaz as a righteous man. It follows that his words and deeds, at least in the telling, would conform to a vision of justice later codified by the Ancients who nurtured that tradition.

First, Boaz asks, "Whose girl is that?" Yet he has already seen that Ruth is a gleaner. From this, we understand that ancient landowners applied a certain proprietary sense to "their" gleaners, who likely came to the fields of a specific owner with some regularity during the harvest seasons. The phrase "whose girl is that?" clearly suggests a special connection which, given the lack of formal employer-employee relationship and the ensuing story, seems to have been one of concern and support (but as well, support that could not discriminate against others who wanted to glean the same field; more on this aspect in chapter 3).

Boaz then counsels Ruth to "stay here close to my girls. Keep your eyes on the field they are reaping and follow them." His advice is critical to Ruth's success in the fields. But Boaz does more than mentor Ruth on strategies to glean productively. He urges her to shadow the reapers. From that vantage she learns the ways of reaping, a skill that could evolve into paid future employment.

Boaz models the behavior of a man respected by the tradition, emphasizing the tzedakah of mentoring and training the untrained for gainful employment as part of the mandated gleaning process.

From Ethics to Advocacy

Today's army of "real unemployed" US workers numbers over twenty-one million. The current economic paradigm remains fixated on unlimited profit as the remedy, despite now-overwhelming evidence that rising profits do not lift all boats. At the same time, temporary unemployment subsidies funded by broad-based taxes—in part by those most likely to become future victims themselves—form the basis of the nominal relief that is offered. And as productivity continues to rise, additional jobs are lost and real-dollar compensation of remaining wage earners falls further behind.

By contrast, Just Market values are focused on creating and sustaining universal employment opportunity. Just Market policies channel employer-funded obligations to create new full-time jobs that expand private sector operations and fund desperately needed public works—roads, bridges, ports, and parks, to name a few. Within the Just Market paradigm, the increasing number of those whose work is reduced or eliminated by productivity advances share in the profits reaped by companies that realize those gains. Just Market policy:

- Supports a *Pe'ah Set-Aside that applies a 1.67% tax on business expenses to fund new jobs* on a company-by-company basis. Where in-house expansion is declined, the company obligation is dedicated to public works labor costs. Over six million new jobs can be projected in the first year of the Set-Aside.

- Establishes a *Shikhekhah Labor Displacement Fund that dedicates one-half of each year's private sector savings from productivity improvement to compensating workers* dislocated by technology advances.

- Dedicates a portion of the Shikhekhah Set-Aside to *incentivize local micro-loan funds and entrepreneurial mentoring* by civic and community organizations.

- *Requires eligible individuals to accept Pe'ah Set-Aside job opportunities* in order to qualify for other public benefits. Eligibility takes into account emotional and physical capability as well as family-driven care obligations.

3. A LEVEL PLAYING FIELD

The Just Market actively promotes healthy, robust competition in three competitive arenas: among businesses; between business and consumers; and within the workforce. But Just Market policies also support a fair playing field and reject competitive tactics that lead to market-controlling entities, price manipulation, and excessive profit margins at the expense of consumers and small business—all subjects covered in this chapter. A related discussion in the chapter 6 review of Sabbatical values looks at the level playing field and the Just Market system of transgenerational wealth transfers.

The Business-to-Business Playing Field

The Ancients embraced a competitive structure as the norm of human economic exchange. Nothing in the texts condemns either wealthy individuals or wealth creation *per se*. But the freedom to compete in order to garner that wealth isn't absolute. When a competitive tactic effectively stifled rather than enhanced competition, the Ancients struggled to find the proper balance of interests:

> Rabbi Yehudah said: A storekeeper must not furnish little children with presents of nuts because he accustoms them to buy all their needs at his place. The Sages, however, permit this (saying), "What is the reason of the rabbis who permit to give presents to children? Because the storekeeper may say to his competitor: 'I distribute nuts; you may do so with plums.'" (BT Bava Metzia 60a)

Rabbi Yehudah declares against business owners offering giveaways. His argument condemns modern loss-leading strategies, since these also "accustom them to buy all their needs at his place." Yet the majority of the Sages shrugged their collective shoulders at this example because it's relatively easy for another small competitor to match: "The storekeeper may say to his competitor: 'I distribute nuts; you may do so with plums.'"

Lower prices helped the poor, at least in the short run. So, when two small shopkeepers were involved in a dispute, the majority sided with lower prices, first in the Oral Law and again in the commentaries of the Gemara.

On the other hand, loss-leading practices could drive ethical shopkeepers out of business. The nub of this issue was left to later commentators, perhaps because the problems inherent in unrealistic giveaways were clarified as larger competitors became a more common factor in the market. Where loss leading is not about a few nuts or plums, but about larger stakes that are beyond the capacity of other competitors, Just Market policy takes account of the difference. In those cases, predatory discounts—loss leading designed to eliminate competition—are considered an aggressive assault on market balance and so, ultimately, on consumers:

> Drastically lowering the price of merchandise is forbidden, because this destroys the market (competition) and causes loss to others . . . It is permitted to do only what others are capable of doing. (*Arukh haShulkhan Hoshen Mishpat* 228:14)

Although consumers are their first concern, the Ancients also recognized that flesh-and-blood merchants who established businesses, built communities, and maintained a personal stake in them had rights that could override those of far-flung economic interests:

> Rav Huna the son of Rav Joshua said: ". . . a resident of one town can prevent the resident of another town from setting up a competing business. However, one who pays taxes in that town cannot be prevented." (BT Bava Batra 21b)

Along the same lines, it is the right of local stakeholders, not of more powerful economic interests, to determine whether additional competitors from outside the community would, on balance, help or hurt its residents:

> The residents of an alley can prevent one another from bringing into their alley a tailor, a tanner, a teacher or other sorts of craft persons, but they

cannot prevent one another from opening up competing businesses. (BT Bava Batra 21b)

The Just Market supports competition and change. But the agent of change also incurs responsibility and obligation. If prices can be incrementally reduced and competition encouraged by the introduction of a new entry into the market, it is welcomed. But if existing businesses cannot compete for reasons that are beyond their control and mainly advantage outside interests, then obligations accrue to compensate economic losers and to develop alternative paths to prosperity for local residents. And where outside merchants are given access, the impacts on local businesses are mitigated by regulation:

> Certain basket-sellers brought baskets ... The townspeople came and stopped them, so they appealed . . . (Rabina) said, "They have come from outside and they can sell to the people from outside." This restriction, however, applied only to the market day, but not to other days; and even on the market day only for selling in the market, but not for going round to the houses. (BT Bava Batra 22a)

Would the Ancients have permitted Walmart to establish a regional center at the hub of several small rural towns? Possibly, but only if economic alternatives were prepared for local businesses affected by the development. Would Walmart have been allowed to operate inside one of those towns? Probably not, although the company's willingness to structure economic alternatives for negatively affected townspeople and merchants might change that equation.

In my first experience as a business owner, I consulted in distressed Rust Belt regions of north central and western Pennsylvania. I worked with a string of towns—Franklin, Clearfield, Dubois, Warren, Corry, and dozens of others you've likely never heard of—all former heavy industrial powerhouses, all silenced by deserted factories. Manufacturing would not likely return, certainly not in the same way, but the locals in every area still struggled to keep their little downtowns vital. And they were losing decisively, storefront by storefront, one hardware or men's clothing shop or pharmacy after another, while Walmarts sprouted at regional hubs and hammered the last nail into the economic coffin that each of those towns had become. It was heartbreaking, completely irreversible "progress." The Just Market would not permit it without demanding compensatory measures for dislocated business owners, employees, and surrounding residents, at the least.

The Walmart example illustrates a larger and growing problem of economic imbalance. Among the Ancients, massive online retailers, for example, would certainly not have been permitted to maintain tax-free advantages over local brick-and-mortar operations that are barred from "what others are capable of doing" as a matter of government policy. Just Market policy would even support local storefront merchants whose services are abused by consumers who fully intend to purchase online but use showrooms to arm themselves with comparative product information. The Ancients conclude that "one should not ask a seller, 'How much does this cost?' if there is no intention to purchase" (BT Bava Metzia 58b).

Just Market policy would consider the difference between outside interests that encourage a developing economy to modernize (typified by tax assistance or other incentives for economically depressed regions, and in some cases by open trade agreements with developing countries), and practices that create impossible hurdles for otherwise viable local businesses (for example, big box retail giants that usurp local markets). To the extent that the big boxes compete beyond "what others can do," squeezing out small competitors and local jobs, there is no ethical value to incorporating their goods and services into a developed economy.

Real people and their communities—commonly cited as beneficiaries of competition—are also placed at economic risk as a result of competitive excess. That a presidential candidate can trumpet Staples' successful campaign to eviscerate local office goods suppliers in the nineties—without bothering to note its toll on local communities, businesses, and downtowns—speaks volumes about the current market paradigm. Just Market values suggest that businesses that "win" by disrupting the level playing field incur obligations to the vanquished as well as the customer base. Stiglitz notes that

> Dominant firms have tools with which to suppress
> competition, and often they can even suppress
> innovation . . . the revenue from which doesn't .
> . . go to public purposes, but rather enriches the
> coffers of the monopolists.[73]

Despite marginally lower retail prices, community after community has experienced significant net losses from the steamroller effect of a tilted playing field. Four studies undertaken between 2007 and 2011 quantified the risk to communities from national chains that drive out small local competitors by operating outside the realm of "doing only what others are capable of doing."

The studies assessed the percentage of local wages, goods, and services derived from the comparative sales of chains and independently owned businesses in Portland, ME; San Francisco, CA; New Orleans, LA; and Grand Rapids, MI. Table 3-1 displays the aggregate percentage of local impact in seven different competitive situations. A Local Advantage Index quantifies the relative impact of independently owned local competitors over chain operations.

Table 3-1. Locally Owned vs. Chain Store Economic Impacts
Local Wages, Procured Goods and Services

	Industry	Economic Impact		Local Advantage
		Chain	Local	
Portland, ME	Dollar Tree/Mixed	33%	58%	1.76x
New Orleans, LA	Target/Mixed	16%	32%	2.03x
Grand Rapids, MI	Restaurants	37%	56%	1.51x
San Francisco, CA	Bookstores	19%	32%	1.70x
San Francisco, CA	Toys	19%	33%	1.72x
San Francisco, CA	Sporting Goods	20%	33%	1.70x
San Francisco, CA	Fast Food	43%	56%	1.30x

Institute for Local Self-Reliance

The incremental benefit of locally owned retailers for community economies ranged from 30% (in the fast-food industry in San Francisco) to over twice as much when a typical Target store was compared to a similar-sized mix of local retailers in New Orleans. Outside of the restaurant industry, each of the four comparisons indicates more than 70% greater community impact on local wages, goods, and services purchased from local merchants.[74] In each of these studies, the value of promoting

local businesses over national chain interests clearly benefits local
stability and prosperity.

To reasonably assess the trade-offs, a Just Market scenario
calls for full disclosure of the likely impacts of additional development or the introduction of large outside competitors. Communities targeted for development by outside businesses have a right
to know the cost-benefit calculation between any proposed new
entry and established businesses that serve the local population. Firms seeking entry into local markets should be obligated
to fund independently conducted studies that clearly compare
impacts on local employment, income, and the procurement of
products and services. After review, communities would maintain the right to deny development permits to outside firms that
cannot demonstrate equal or larger local impacts. Where new
entrants are permitted to develop, they would become responsible for reemployment or compensation of those who are sepa-
rated from their means of livelihood as a result. Loss-leading as a
strategy to drive competition out of business (to do "what others
cannot do") would be outlawed as an unfair competitive practice.

Fair Play in the Workplace

The requirement for fair and equitable treatment of all people is
central to the Just Market ethic, which specifically requires that
foreign and minority workers must be treated without discrimination under the law:

> You and the stranger will be alike before the Lord;
> the same ritual and the same rule shall apply to
> you and to the stranger who resides among you.
> (Numbers 15:16)

The same ethic is rendered even more precisely in Leviticus 19:34, which demands that "The stranger who resides with you shall be to you as one of your citizens." Yet it's axiomatic that the core texts of Western theology call repeatedly for special attention to the widow, the orphan, and the stranger—biblical shorthand for disadvantaged and oppressed classes:

> When you gather the grapes of your vineyard, do not pick it over again; that shall be for the stranger, the fatherless, and the widow . . . (Deuteronomy 24:21, see also 24:20)

So which is it? "One law for all" or special treatment for classes of people that would otherwise be denied meaningful access to the competitive field? In fact, the two go hand in hand. Only when all groups share reasonably similar access to the playing field can there be said to be "one law . . . for you and for the stranger."

Just Market values suggest that "equal" in a literal sense does not always mean "fair" or "level." In the source texts, disadvantaged classes of people legitimately benefit from special mechanisms designed to compensate for extraordinarily difficult situations. Such classes include the poor, the disabled, the aged, and "the stranger," a classification that extends to racial and national minorities.

The commitment to provide meaningful opportunity for disadvantaged classes of people also surfaces in the Talmudic discussion of the gleaning process. The Sages discuss the phrase "after the last of the poor had gone," which describes the point at which the gleaning fields are thrown open to those who are not poor. They assure gleaning rights to even the oldest and physically infirm who must "grope" their way through the fields:

> From what time are (other) people allowed to appropriate the gleanings (of a reaped field)? (The Mishnah tells us) after the "gropers" have gone through it. And so we asked: What is meant by the "gropers"? And Rav Yokhanan answered, "Old people who walk leaning on a stick," while Resh Lekish answered, "The last in the succession of gleaners." (BT Bava Metzia 21b)

Consistent with the rules of gleaning the fields, public access was prohibited until after the first pass of those gleaners who were the "weakest of the poor":

> From when is everyone permitted to glean? When the weakest of the poor have made their search.
> (BT Bava Metzia 21b)

Just as Torah and Mishnah Pe'ah create special employment opportunities for the poor and oppressed classes, Just Market mechanisms activate those values by institutionalizing special entry advantages for disadvantaged classes of people, including physically challenged and elder populations, as well as those who have suffered employment barriers due to race, class, nationality, and gender.

Minority populations in the US are among the economically burdened descendants of the oppressed "strangers" cited in the ancient texts. In every measurement category, African-American and Hispanic unemployment rates are today, and historically have been, 50% to 85% higher than those of the general population. In the US, large gaps remain even as recovery from the 2008 recession slowly continues (table 3-2). The reasons may be complex, but wage gaps require address—and jobs.

Table 3-2. Racial Unemployment Rate Index

	July-12	July-13	Index
White	8.1	6.9	1.00
African American	14.0	12.7	1.84
Latino	11.4	10.4	1.51

US Bureau of Labor Statistics

(White unemployment rate= 1.00)

When employment *is* made available, the same classes of people (as well as women) suffer from extensive wage gap disparity relative to the dominant white male population in the US. In 2013, the average wage of Hispanic workers was almost 30% less than those earned by white men, while black male wages were fully 25% lower than those of male whites.[75] In Israel, wages of Jews of Ethiopian origin and Israeli Arabs are about 40% lower than those of native-born Israeli Jews and immigrants from the former Soviet Union during the first year of employment in high-earner professions. That gap widens to 64% after ten years.[76]

Current US affirmative action protections require compliance from business operations covering approximately twenty-six million employees, or nearly 22% of the total civilian workforce (92,500 non-construction establishments and 100,000 construction establishments). These contractors and subcontractors are required to "take affirmative action to ensure that all individuals have an equal opportunity for employment, without regard to race, color, religion, sex, national origin, disability or status as a Vietnam era or special disabled veteran."[77] The rest of the economy (approximately 90% of business establishments and 78% of the workforce) is exempt.

Like the Ancients, the Just Market responds to these levels of disparity by expanding tools that it already knows have succeeded with the 22% "sample population" covered by affirmative action. The extension of similar guidelines to all employers of the federally predetermined scale is a logical next step in support of the values of the fair playing field. Stiglitz sums it up well yet again: "Even if we were successful in eliminating discrimination today, its consequences would still be with us. Fortunately, we've learned how to improve matters through affirmative action programs."[78]

A Level Playing Field on the Job

The Ancients extended their concern for the well-being of disadvantaged and discriminated groups in Leviticus and Deuteronomy to condemn favoritism, cronyism, and nepotism. In general, Jewish tradition upholds the protection of family before community, and of community before the outside world (BT Bava Metzia 71a). But in this passage, Talmud stipulates a fair and level economic playing field on the job:

> A landowner may not hire a man to work on his field and have the man's son glean after him.[79] One who does not allow the poor to glean, or allows

one, and not another, or helps one (to the detriment of the other), indeed, he openly steals from the poor. (Mishnah Pe'ah 5:6)

This in no way contradicts the Torah's guidance that downtrodden classes of people deserve special compensatory treatment.[80] It does suggest that, those special conditions aside, favoritism and nepotism, along with collective forms of discrimination, are considered "stealing from the poor" and should not be tolerated. As for application to contemporary society, Paul Krugman concludes that

America actually stands out as the advanced country in which it matters most who your parents were, the country in which those born on one of society's lower rungs have the least chance of climbing to the top or even to the middle.[81]

In the Book of Ruth, Boaz assures Ruth that "I have ordered the men not to molest you." He issues a set of unambiguous orders to his laborers. They must not only desist from harassing Ruth, but also actively aid her no doubt clumsy initial efforts at gleaning by throwing a few extra sheaves her way:

You are not only to let her glean among the sheaves, without interference, but you must also pull some stalks out of the heaps and leave them for her to glean, and not scold her. (Ruth 2:15–16)

That night, after eating of Ruth's bounty from the field, Naomi advises her to glean with Boaz again: "It is best, daughter, that you go out with his girls and not be annoyed in some other field" (Ruth 2:22). It would seem that other landowners are not as supportive toward gleaners, underscoring the value of the fair treatment that those in Boaz's field can expect.

Playing by the Rules

Will playing by the rules of competitive fairness debilitate the society that attempts it? The Just Market offers a protection: the level playing field applies only to those who accept its values. For those who attempt to take advantage of Just Market practices without adopting them as their own, the rules of economic engagement are different.

In the Torah discussion of debt release, the Jew is enjoined to treat another Jew (*akh* or brother) who has fallen on hard times as he would a resident gentile (*toshav*) whose status is that of a workman rather than a slave (Leviticus 25:39). The call implies respectful treatment of the Other who upholds civilized social values, and endows him with rights, not only privileges, under the law. Debts due from the foreign settler (*ger toshav*) are annulled for the "brother" and non-kinsman gentile ("neighbor") alike at the Sabbatical Year (Deuteronomy 15:2).

But when discussing those from outside the community who play by rules that are very different, the prohibition on exacting debt during the Sabbatical Year is reversed:

> You may dun the foreigner (*nokhri*), but you must
> remit whatever is due you from your kinsmen.
> (Deuteronomy 15:3)

By using the word "nokhri" rather than "ger" or "ger toshav," the text denotes a temporary visitor for trade purposes, whose own civilization does not embrace restrictions on debt or interest, whether during the Sabbatical Year or at other times. The nokhri plays by other rules. The Just Market does not obligate its advocates to engage with one hand tied behind their backs.

From Ethics to Advocacy

Just Market policy toward the level playing field is centered on sustaining viable communities and the ability of their populations to access the "necessities of life." It balances business-to-business competition in the consumer interest, both short and long term. But the Just Market also provides protection for small local businesses whose social instincts and history more reliably support local communities. From that perspective, Just Market policies take into account differences of scale among competitors and their effect on the communities in which they do business.

The Just Market also recognizes the needs and rights of both individuals and diverse population segments to compete on a level playing field. When dealing with issues of competition and discrimination within the workforce, maintaining a level playing field often means balancing the interests of individuals in need against disadvantaged classes of people. Just Market policies that promote the creation of a level playing field include:

- Instituting commercial laws to *prohibit predatory loss leader tactics*.

- Obligating incoming non-resident businesses to fund government-sponsored impact studies and *submit compensatory proposals for businesses and employees likely to be dislocated* by new operations.

- *Expanding affirmative action coverage* to all private businesses as well as government contractors.

4. COMMERCIAL AND PROMOTIONAL INTEGRITY

The Just Market is comprised of transactions between individuals. Like other healthy social interactions, those transactions should be based on honest, straightforward relationships. Modern capitalism also formally supports the need for fraud-free relationships. But, as we are reminded almost daily in the headlines, the commitment of various free-market societies to enforcing that value varies enormously.

Intolerance of commercial fraud speaks to the respect of one person for another, whether based on the secular belief that we live as equals on earth, or, for the spiritually inclined, that we are all created *b'tselem Elohim*, in the image of the divinity.

In the texts of the Ancients, fraud includes commercial cheating or concealment of any sort; any misleading activity or misleading promotion of any product or process; any artificial price manipulation against the interests of consumers; and any actions or impressions designed to mislead buyers about the nature or character of a product or a service—or about its purveyor. Economist William L. Black characterizes fraud in a strikingly similar manner.

Fraud is deceit. And the essence of fraud is, "I create trust in you, and then I betray that trust, and get you to give me something of value." And as a result, there's no more effective acid against trust than fraud, especially fraud by top elites, and that's what we have.[82]

The Ancients' emphasis on precise, honest measures and transparent transactions suggests three motivating elements that attach to the commercial process as a matter of historical need and ethic.

First, the Oral Law itself developed during protracted periods of Jewish nation building. After the destruction of the first Temple, successive Jewish leaderships struggled to unify a fractured people during periods of colonial rule. A just, comprehensible commercial law promoted trade and trust among Jewish communities that were geographically isolated enough to have developed diverse day-to-day commercial practices.

Second, honest measures reflect an individual's trustworthiness and reliability—to the law and to the community. Detailed procedures for selecting and maintaining materials for scales and weights protected the consumer first and foremost.[83] But excruciatingly specific obligations also protected the merchant, who might otherwise be tempted to stray from honest practices—reminiscent of the reasoning behind the requirement for early designation of the pe'ah gleaning portion of the field. As well, stringent regulation of market transactions protected honest merchants who would otherwise fall victim to unfair competitive practices, since the dishonest margins created by fraud could be expended on loss-leader pricing intended to drive competition from the market.

Third, Jewish law was designed, in part, to address social inequity. Just as the laws of gleaning generally favored the landless at the expense of the landowner, and the poor at the expense of the rich, the Ancients' commercial commentary generally favored the consumer over the merchant, the commercially unsophisticated over the conversant, and the interests of the man-in-the-street over the well-to-do.

> . . . a storekeeper must allow the side of the scale with product to sink a handbreadth lower than the side of the scale with the weights. (BT Bava Batra 88b)

Transactional Fraud

The pe'ah requirement for landowners to precisely delineate gleaning sections of their fields and orchards early in the season was designed to thwart the temptation to scout for low-yield sections just before the harvest. That same skepticism pervaded the Ancients' assessment of fraud.

Ancient texts placed three responsibilities on merchants when it came to assessing weights: to weigh their product honestly; to scrupulously maintain the integrity of commercial tools such as scales (or, in modernity, accounts); and to assure that the transactional process provided the buyer (or other less sophisticated party) a high level of comfort and trust. As a result, locally familiar methods prevailed in the commercial process.

> In places where it is customary to use small measures, one may not use large ones. Where it

is customary to use large measures, one may not use small ones. In places where it is customary to level the measure, one may not heap it. Where it is customary to heap it, one may not level it. (BT Bava Batra 88a–b)

In addition to demanding a measurement process that was transparent and easily understood by the customer, the Ancients specified preventive measures that reflected the varying levels of precision needed for small and larger transactions:

Wholesalers must clean their measures once in thirty days . . . Storekeepers must clean their measures twice a week, wipe their weights once a week and wipe their scales for every weighing. (BT Bava Batra 88a–b)

As for intent, what's included in a transaction is often implied by the price. The Just Market imposes a standard of reasonability when determining disputes.

He who sold a wagon has not sold the mules. He who sold the mules has not sold the wagon. He who sold the yoke has not sold the oxen. He who sold the oxen has not sold the yoke. Rabbi Judah says: The price indicates. How? If he said, "Sell me your yoke for 200 *zuz*, it is obvious that a yoke (by itself) is not sold for 200 zuz." But the Sages say: The price is no proof . . . (Later Sages add): But if the price is no proof, cancellation of the purchase should follow. (BT Bava Batra 77b)

The Ancients draw on two key Torah texts to regulate against false or careless weights and measures:

> You shall not falsify measures of length, weight, or capacity . . . You shall have an honest balance, honest weights, an honest ephah and an honest *hin*. (Leviticus 19:35–36) . . . You shall not have in your pouch alternate weights, larger and smaller. You shall not have in your house alternate measures, a larger and a smaller. You must have completely honest weights and completely honest measures. (Deuteronomy 25:13–16)

Indeed, the core fairness of commercial exchange is deemed so important in the tradition that while a merchant's accidental or trivial mistakes can be forgiven, they must be compensated, no matter how small, by whichever party benefited from the error.

> If one sells commodities to another by measure or by weight or by number and has made even the slightest error, the difference must always be returned. Thus, if one has sold to another one hundred nuts for a *denar* and it is found that there were one hundred and one or ninety-nine, the transaction is valid, but the amount of the error must be returned to the aggrieved party. (Maimonides, *Laws of Sale* 15:1)

There are only two possible reasons to devote so much attention to such minute transactional processes.

One is that a significant proportion of consumers lived at the very edge of the financial precipice. The Ancients understood their need for each and every almond or pistachio that the common man purchased.

The other is that the ethics of the marketplace mirror the core of human relationships. Jews live as individuals to be sure, but as individuals who profoundly reflect the values of families and communities. One of those values was—and still should be—the choice of ethical commercial behavior over petty gain. With that choice, we recognize each other's right to survive and prosper. Those who step over the line of honest business behavior threaten the community bond.

> If one has sold something . . . and a defect is later found on the purchased article, the purchaser may return the article (and be compensated) even after the lapse of many years because this was a transaction in error. (Maimonides, *Laws of Sale* 15:1)

The Ancients went even further, suggesting that the deliberate, regular use of unjust measures or weights—that is, of fraud in the course of commercial activity—constitutes a crime on the same level as sexual immorality:

> Rabbi Levi said: The punishment for transgressing the law of measures is harsher than the transgressions of incest. In the latter one can repent, whereas in the former, it is not possible to repent. (BT Bava Batra 88b)

Why would this be? Maimonides suggests a possibility that is consistent with the larger traditional Jewish view on evil acts: "The latter (sexual immorality) may be a sin against God only, the former (false weights) against one's fellow man" (Maimonides, *Laws of Theft* 7:12). While this reasoning reflects a medieval lack of concern for the (usually female) victim that borders on the creepy to modern ears, it also emphasizes just how seriously fraud is considered in the tradition.

David Saelman, an engineer in Israel's hi-tech sector, draws out the implications of this issue:

> One who violates the laws of sexual conduct has the ability to fully repent for his transgression by abstaining and making a vow (to the victim) not to repeat the act . . . However, a merchant who has deceived many customers over time by purposely using altered weights in his business transactions will not remember how much money he had stolen and from whom he had stolen.[84]

More than any one act, this inexorably expanding circle of victims triggered the Ancients' severe response to fraud. Even then, they recognized the link between fraud and social disintegration. Their discussion consequently covered not only the mechanics of weights and measures, but all manner of commercial subterfuge and attempts to mislead about the quantity, quality, benefits, or origin of products and services.

Concealment and Promotional Fraud

Just Market consideration of fraud ranges from its most blatant forms to subtle commercial enticements. The seemingly archaic case studies reviewed by the Ancients are easily ridiculed or excerpted to dismiss Talmudic "irrelevance" to modern life. In fact, the tradition's observations of market misrepresentation are, so to speak, right on the money. The frauds of ancient times are replicated in practices familiar to, and quite often accepted by, contemporary society as a matter of course.

> A seller may not sift crushed beans to remove the refuse. These are the words of Abba Shaul. But the Sages allow it. However, they agree that the seller may not sift just at the opening of the bin, for this would be deception. (BT Bava Metzia 59b–60a)

Naturally, the Ancients teach, a merchant can improve his stock by hulling or removing refuse. But he is forbidden to arrange only the processed beans at the top merely to trick people into thinking that the stock under the visible goods is in the same pristine condition. Contrast this to the now-common practice of rearranging or mislabeling foods in the supermarket so that the consumer believes she is purchasing a more expensive or higher-quality item![85]

Promotion that distracts from the nature of a product is fraud, even if the misrepresentation has little or no impact on its intended victim:

> One may not stiffen an animal's hair, nor enlarge an animal's intestines; nor may one soak meat in

water . . . One must not sell to a non-Jew meat
of an animal not slaughtered according to ritual
law under the impression that it is meat from
an animal slaughtered according to ritual law,
although to the non-Jew, the two are the same.
(Maimonides, *Laws of Sale*, 18:3)

"Buyer beware" is a concept that held little sway among
the Sages. Even as Just Market policy demands restitution for
product defects discovered years after a sale, it also requires a
forthright declaration of fact before the completion of any transaction:

It is forbidden to deceive people in buying and
selling or to deceive them by creating a false
impression . . . If one knows that an article he
is selling has a defect, he must inform the buyer
about it. It is forbidden to deceive people even by
words. (Maimonides, *Laws of Sale*, 18:1)

This original demand for "full disclosure" ripples beyond
the immediate transaction, encompassing the social relations that
surround and spur on the deal. Is there honest and full disclosure?
Does silence obstruct it? Does an assault on the senses lead the
unwary to expect a product or service of one type, when in fact it
is something else? On all this, the Ancients passed down observations on fraudulent practices that are today as commonplace as
they are harmful.

Retraction for Gain

In addition to the issues surrounding retracted labor-management agreements discussed in chapter 5, the Ancients condemn breaking business contracts for gain. In a telling vignette mentioned in the introduction, the Sages review the story of Rav Khiyya bar Yosef, a Talmudic commentator, who was threatened with a steep penalty for attempting to renege on a deal in order to increase his profit:

Rav Khiyya bar Yosef proposes to sell a measure of salt to a buyer. A price is agreed, but Rav Khiyya attempts to alter the deal:

> . . . money was given to Rav Khiyya as advance payment for the salt. Before the delivery, salt rose in price. Rav Khiyya then came before Rav Yokhanan, who ordered him to deliver the salt at the price which was fixed, or submit to the curse (of the Sages) . . . Since only a deposit had been paid, Rav Khiyya bar Yosef thought that the buyer was entitled only to the value of the deposit (at the earlier, lower price). But Rav Yokhanan told him that the buyer was entitled to the entire purchase at the originally agreed-upon price. (BT Bava Metzia 48b)[86]

Rav Khiyya asserts that he should be permitted to retract his word and split a windfall increase in the price of salt with his customer. But Rav Yokhanan suggests that even if Rav Khiyya were technically entitled to abrogate the agreement, he is treading on morally squishy turf and "you must submit to the curse" of the Sages.

"Imposters" and Market Manipulation

We've already seen that the Ancients equated speculators and hoarders with "impostors" who artificially manipulated prices to create excessive profits (BT Bava Batra 89a). The deliberate market distortion inherent in those practices is a close cousin of what the Ancients considered fraud. Likewise, when modern investment banks are given free rein to control commodity logistics, warehousing, and finance while engaging in speculation around the same product, the risk posed by "impostors" is compounded.

In the US, for example, the aggressive combination of banks and commodity operations has resulted in soaring profits at the expense of business customers and consumers alike, to the benefit of many of the same financial institutions entangled in the mortgage mess. Several of the nation's largest banks, including Goldman Sachs and JP Morgan, have become major players in commodities markets—not only commodity stocks—by investing in huge warehousing operations. In the aluminum market, at least, those operations increase profits through cartel rules that actually reward delays in delivery, profiting the banks even while they trade on internal commodity information at the investment end of the market.[87]

The Ancients were skeptical of wholesalers in the first place; most favored a complete ban on wholesale profit-taking (BT Bava Batra 91a). They reasoned that middlemen added no value and simply made it more difficult for the poor to access the necessities of life.

Today, of course, many wholesale and logistics operations are much more complex and often do provide value-added service at varying levels. But what *hasn't* changed since the days of the Sages is the inclination of those who corner commodity markets to hoard and speculate, manipulating supplies, driving up prices and—in the modern version—enhancing their stock holdings with inside information. The Ancients outlawed "impostors" and installed price controls to keep them at bay. Obviously, our modern view of "impostors" lags far behind.

The Banality of Fraud: Stealing the Mind

Brightly colored cans of alcoholic drinks, obscure clauses in long legal documents, dicey health and beauty claims, "pre-frozen" fish weighed in its iced state or sold as a more expensive species, smaller volumes of cereal in a box whose size doesn't change—these are annoyances replicated day after day that we have come to accept, almost as a nuisance tax for living in the relative comfort (for some) of modern capitalism. All would likely have been classified as fraud in Talmudic-era courts. The Ancients would certainly have called it fraud to sell a box of pistachio pudding with no pistachios. They would have penalized the maker of a package of sliced cheese with the blurb "More Slices!" when the total amount of cheese has been cut; or the seller of a box of crackers with outsized red letters that proclaim "BIG" when the box contains less product by volume than it had in its original package. Yet it's done all the time at your supermarket and mine.[88]

Contemporary fraud includes ancient scams as simple as face-to-face cheating with measures and weights. From there it expands to more sophisticated ploys perpetrated against larger numbers of victims—unwary buyers of products in those increasingly empty boxes and misleading containers, for example.

Spurred by exploding numbers of media outlets (and hence exploding channels of advertising space), increasing numbers of people are lured to improve their attractiveness, prestige, or sex lives, leading them to waste money and hope on fantasy solutions that depersonalize human beings *b'tselem akher* (in the image of another) rather than seeking meaningful growth *b'tselem Elohim* (in the image of the divinity). Technology amplifies the opportunity to create and promote these and other misrepresentations to enormous audiences rather than the crowds of dozens or hundreds prevalent in earlier times. And again, in the eyes of the tradition, the wider the circle, the more grievous the damage and the worse the transgression.

As recent experience in the financial markets has shown, commercial fraud can also take the form of higher-stakes deception that rocks the foundations of an economy—dangerous mortgage terms promised to uncomprehending couples with unrealistic dreams, for example, or hedge funds that have banks betting against their own loans.

The Just Market also condemns schemes—commercial and political—that create a false sense of quality and desirability. The tradition classifies these as "stealing the mind" of another human being (*g'nivat da'at*), the most despicable of the seven forms of thievery (Tosefta Bava Kama 7:3; Tosefta Bava Metzia 3:15). G'nivat da'at includes subtle forms of fraud: misleading people through smooth talk, splashy promotions, and environments meant to create a sense of quality or hope that is not consistent with the product, scam, or personality that is being sold.

In the modern world, g'nivat da'at has exploded in the form of fraud that is perpetrated anonymously during the delivery of abstract and financial services. These thefts take place far from the consumer's eyes. They are exemplified by stock manipulation and Ponzi schemes, often using a carefully culti-

vated reputation to entice investors into fraudulent pyramids.[89]
The betrayal of community trust inherent in much of this type of
fraud compounds the violation.

Even the promotion of personal character can serve as
a stage for g'nivat da'at, including fraudulent representation by
hucksters and politicians who market themselves for gain or evil.
This most egregious level of fraud relies on a convincing public
persona that straddles the murky modern nexus of commerce,
politics, and celebrity. It is exemplified by the politician whose
prestige relies on demagogic "values" but whose lack of personal
ethics betrays the trust he has won to render decisions on all
manner of commercial and social policy. Here the "false market"
is the impostor himself. His "product" is wholly a fraud foisted
quite personally on millions of people. By Just Market standards,
this level of fraud surpasses all others and merits commensurate
penalties. Yet its perpetrators are often among the most privileged
and protected individuals of our age.

In the modern market, the more remote the fraud or theft,
the lighter the penalty is likely to be. This reluctance to prosecute
white-collar and professional crime, despite the immense harm it
inflicts on individuals and society, turns the Just Market value on
its head.

Commenting on the same issue, Jonathan Zell, a former
special assistant to the US attorney for the Southern District of
Ohio, notes that

> Except in the most egregious cases or where the
> larger interests of the industry are involved, execu-
> tives and professionals are usually charged only
> civilly, which means they pay a fine or lose some

privilege (often just temporarily). For this purpose, an alphabet soup of regulatory agencies, whose real purpose is to protect the industries, exists.[90]

With the authoritative experience of a prosecutor, Zell goes on to suggest that "Stockbrokers who engage in unauthorized trading; (and) manufacturers that sell harmful products and then lie about their safety . . . are treated lightly by the courts when complaints against them are even registered."[91]

The consistently light slap of the courts against fraud is tantamount to official support. As *New York Times* columnist Joe Nocera points out regarding the conduct of banking giant HSBC:

> Who knew that the British bank was the favored institution of money launderers everywhere? As it turns out, the Senate Permanent Investigations subcommittee knew . . . Twice before, in 2003 and 2007, the bank had been cited by regulators for what *The Times* described as "extensive money laundering ways." Despite the reprimands, it continued to do business with banks that laundered money for drug traffickers and institutions suspected of having ties to terrorists.[92]

Yet the fraudulent practices of HSBC (and other megabanks whose scandalous practices now seem to surface with alarming regularity) pales next to the LIBOR scandal, which was essentially a conspiracy of major banks to manipulate interest rates by fraudulently answering a single daily question from the British Bankers Association: "At what rate could you borrow funds, were you to do so by asking for and then accepting inter-bank offers in a reasonable market size just prior to eleven a.m.?" Lenders develop interest rates based on the responses. As Tim Lee of the conservative *US News & World Report* puts it, "The LIBOR interest rates set the cost of borrowing." He goes on to say that

> ... it almost feels ridiculous to be surprised or even outraged that there has been "manipulation" in these figures ... (I)t also seems naïve to think that large banks driven mostly by next quarter's earnings would do anything other than maximize their profits at every turn ... (T)he really concerning part of this story is not that big banks were giving market numbers which were not 100 percent accurate, but rather that they were colluding to set interest rates and thereby create opportunities for profits from trading with this information.[93]

Is the stringent Just Market attitude toward fraud still relevant today? You bet it is.

From Ethics to Advocacy

Whether it's insider trading, mortgage companies betting on loans to fail, or banks colluding to fix interest rates, financial and commercial scandals seem to sprout daily on the front pages. Perhaps even more distressing are the commonplace character frauds that run the gamut from confidence schemes to politicians trading on fake resumes, fake war hero experience, and fake morality. The unwillingness of the current free market to thoroughly roust fraud results in millions of routinely cheated investors and consumers, as well as citizens who are taken in by the hucksters who represent them in government.

Modern Just Market policy supports the equalization of penalties for common theft, commercial fraud, and character fraud in the public sphere. Variations in penalties are dependent only on the breadth and volume of damages. This means, for example, that financial thieves would no longer receive sentencing privileges over "common" thieves; and that misleading promotion of products, services, or opportunities would be judged along with other forms of "theft of the mind" as stealing rather than clever marketing. Fraud penalties would be established for public officials and politicians who lie or mislead the public regarding their character, background, or resumes. Just Market policy leads to advocacy in five categories:

- Assuring the *integrity and transparency of commercial tools, instruments, and services.*

- *Requiring universal rights to return defective property* without cost.

- *Requiring clear promotional and packaging language* including notice of altered size, volume, and product quality.

- *Eliminating the corporate fraud shield and legislating personal criminal liability* for these and other forms of commercial and public character fraud.

- *Classifying misleading promotion (g'nivat da'at) as a form of criminal fraud* in both commerce and the public sector that governs it.

5. RESPECT FOR LABOR

In her 2010 essay, "Servants to Servants or Servants to God," Rabbi Jill Jacobs suggests that "(i)n the halakhic ideal, the employer and employee become equal partners, each of whom has responsibilities toward the other, and each of whom benefits from the other."[94]

True enough. But even in the ancient period, it was obvious that there was something unique and intrinsically loaded about the employer-employee relationship. The Sages discerned the need for ground rules to govern the peculiar set of human interactions that today we call labor relations.

The source texts denote two different types of workers. One is generally skilled, a tradesman or jobber who applies his knowledge and tools to a specific project for which he is paid a fixed sum. The other type is a semiskilled or menial wage worker who might be paid on either a task or time basis.

The tradesman maintains his own business, accounts, tools, and possibly a shop. As the literal meaning of the Hebrew category name indicates (*kablan*, literally "receiver"), the tradesman is normally distinguished by the application of a value-added process on received goods, or by a product he develops through his labor, skill, and tools. Payment is made at the completion of a work phase or an entire project.

The *po'el*, or laborer, may be a day worker, akin to modern casual workers who congregate on corners familiar to construction, warehouse, and landscape contractors throughout the United States and Israel. Alternatively, he may be a longer-term hired hand. The fortunate po'el's work may be seasonally repetitive, synched to the routine of a specific foreman or owner. Recall Boaz's reference to his reapers as "my girls."

Because the nature of trade work was project-specific, the Ancients applied commercial ethics to many elements of the relationship between craftsman and customer. But the inherent love-hate aspect of the employer-employee relationship also led them to develop an additional set of operating principles that, even in Talmudic times, suggested a specialized understanding of the labor exchange.

As we've seen, Ruth, Mishnah Pe'ah, and the source texts in Deuteronomy and Leviticus introduced value sets that are integral to the Jewish guide to labor relations: mutually respectful behaviors; condemnation of favoritism and nepotism; fair treatment of foreign workers and others who are not part of the dominant culture. But beyond those tone-setting issues, the Ancients articulate requirements for the employer-employee relationship that are clear, specific, and as easily recognizable today as they were in the third or fourth century. For the most part, these are not the character-based ethics that we encountered in discussions of commercial transactions in the previous chapter. Instead, they focus on proprietors and hired subordinates who perform the work necessary to create wealth for an owner in an environment that previewed modern capitalist operations.

An Uneasy Peace

The Ancients were acutely aware of the power that employers held over the workers they engaged. They comment at length on two of its manifestations—the drive to depress labor costs and increase profit; and the inclination to erode employees' self-respect as a means of maintaining control over wages and conditions.

The Sages engage in a conversation regarding the meaning of the terms "oppress" and "rob" as they apply to the prohibitions against poor treatment of workers. They set up the discussion by quoting from Torah:

> You shall not coerce your neighbor. You shall not commit robbery. The wages of a laborer shall not remain with you until morning. (Leviticus 19:13)

Directly addressing employers, the Sages declare that hired laborers, who are considered a subset of "your neighbor(s)," are to be neither oppressed nor robbed in the specific context of their employment. Since the tradition maintains that each word of Torah holds a distinct meaning, the Sages conclude that there must be a difference between "oppression" and "robbery" of an employee, and ask, "What is meant by 'oppression' and 'robbery'?" There are three responses. In the first, Rav Hisda portrays an employer whose delays waste the worker's time by forcing him to return repeatedly to ask for wages that are due him:

Rav Hisda said: "'Go, and come again, go and come again'—that is oppression; 'You have indeed a charge upon me, but I will not pay it'—that is robbery." (BT Bava Metzia 111a)

Rav Hisda describes robbery as an economic crime; the employer acknowledges his contract with the worker and his liability to pay—but refuses to honor his obligation. His definition of oppression, though, is entirely different. "Go, and come again, go and come again" disrespects the worker, playing with his time and emotions by forcing him to return repeatedly and beg for what is his by right.

Rav Sheshet's definition of robbery is almost identical to Hisda's. And like Hisda, his understanding of oppression is personalized. Here the employer's disingenuous assertion that "I have paid you" strikes at the core of the employee's self-respect. It is a blatant negation of his humanity by a statement that both parties know to be patently false:

"But," said Rav Sheshet, "'I have paid you'—that is oppression; 'You have indeed a charge upon me but I will not pay you'—that is robbery." (BT Bava Metzia 111a)

Finally, Rav Abaye equates the dishonest "I paid you" with robbery on its face. But his understanding of oppression aligns with that of the other two Sages. As he sees it, the owner negates the employee's human value by declaring that there was neither an agreement nor a relationship worth recognizing. "I never engaged you," asserts the employer, who in effect says, "You and your claims simply do not exist."

But, said Abaye, "I never engaged you"—that is "oppression"; "I paid you"—that is "robbery." (BT Bava Metzia 111a)

The inclination of many employers to degrade employees as a tool of profit or control is a long-standing and continuing reality. That tendency, along with the imbalance of power inherent in the relationship, inclined the Ancients to give workers the benefit of the doubt in most situations, much as they gave gleaners the benefit of doubt in Mishnah Pe'ah and consumers the benefit of doubt in the transaction process. Even as they attempted to guide the relationship in a just and peaceable direction, the Ancients recognized the likelihood of conflict.

The Sages decry deceitful practices regarding wage determination and payment, as well as ploys that compel workers to labor longer or harder without higher compensation. Conversely, they chide employees who dawdle on company time (BT Bava Metzia 83a, 89a, 89b). When it comes to the employer's obligation to feed employees during the work day, the Talmud hardly sees the exchange as one between gracious host and grateful guest. Rather, the Sages matter-of-factly note that each can be expected to look out for his own interest:

An employer may give his employees wine to drink, that they should not eat many grapes; On the other hand, the laborers may dip their bread in brine, that they should eat many grapes! (BT Bava Metzia 89a)

That is, expect an employer to scheme, even while he provides refreshment to his workers and satisfies the letter of the law. Expect employees to return the favor.

Following the same logical thread, the Sages discuss whether to place a limit on the quantity of an employer's crop that a laborer may eat during work hours:

> (Mishnah): A laborer may eat cucumbers, even to
> the value of a *denar*, or dates, even to the value of a
> *denar*. Rav Elazar Hisma said, "A laborer must not
> eat more than his wage." But the Sages permit it,
> yet one is advised not to be greedy. . . (Gemara):
> They differ as to whether the laborer is advised not
> to be greedy. (Rav Elazar Hisma) holds that he is
> not advised (to be greedy); but the Rabbis main-
> tain that he is. (BT Bava Metzia 92a)

The majority ("the Rabbis") encourage the worker to take what he can under the law, assuming that he will, in turn, fall victim to selfish behavior. Likewise, when a farmhand makes use of his right to eat from the crops that he tends or harvests, the Ancients encourage him to look for the best of the pickings—as long as he doesn't abuse his employer by spending too much time doing so. Questioning whether an employee is permitted to enhance his hunger and the taste of his pickings in order to eat more, they comment:

> As for making the man fit (to eat more), there is
> no question. Our problem is only whether the food
> may be rendered more appetizing . . . Laborers may

eat the top most grapes of the rows[95]—but must not parch them at the fire. (The prohibition) is on account of loss of time. (BT Bava Metzia 89b)

The explanation that "this is on account of loss of time" limits the absolute right of employees, in the interests of efficiency, to eat from the owner's crops while at work. The employee may eat what he likes, but the employer should be assured of a fair day's work in exchange for agreed-upon wages and benefits. This is in keeping with the tradition's determination to balance just treatment with the demands of a competitive environment.

These required minimum behaviors contrast sharply with the more highly honored behavior modeled by Boaz in the Book of Ruth. In addition to guiding her to successful gleaning practices, Boaz offers her water and nourishment in his tent throughout the hot, difficult day: "When you are thirsty, go to the jars and drink some water" (Ruth 2:9). Later, still in the fields, he invites her into his tent: "Come over here and partake of the meal, and dip your morsel in vinegar" (Ruth 2:14).

The Value of Time

In the modern economy, time is a product. It is sold by the employee to the employer at a price. Once the employee enters into the arrangement, she retains ownership, but not control, over her time. Modern labor laws commonly mandate that the price of labor must increase with extended hours or extra days, but the legal prerogative of the employer to manipulate the workday, compel work on weekends, or even enforce random schedules is for the most part unquestioned.

The Ancients articulate a different view. Work hours that extend the standard day cannot be compelled, with or without incentives. Idle time or cancelled work due to employer negligence must be compensated. These and other laws don't hinge on a union contract; they stem directly from the Jewish social contract.

The Ancients assured that employees who are promised work will receive it—or be compensated for their loss if the employer retracts:

> ... (I)f ass-drivers are engaged to convey a load of grain from a certain place and go there and find no grain, or if laborers (hired to plough a field) go and find the field a swamp (unfit for plowing), the employer must pay them in full. (BT Bava Metzia 76b)

As a matter of Jewish ethic, one person's time is as valuable as another's, regardless of station in life. With such a worldview, the Ancients were no doubt perplexed by the cavalier manner with which some employers would—and do—assume effective control over the time of other beings (BT Bava Metzia 111a; BT Bava Metzia 58b). The same principle no doubt stiffened the requirement to pay workers at the end of each day's labor, a law asserted twice in Torah:

> You shall not abuse a needy and destitute laborer, whether a fellow countryman or a non-citizen in your communities. You must pay him his wages on the same day, before the sun sets, for he is needy

and urgently depends on it; else he will cry to the
Lord against you and you will incur guilt. (Deuteronomy 24:14–15)[96]

This verse, and the several Talmudic exchanges that clarify
and reinforce it, can be meaningfully taken at face value. Wages
should be paid, and paid promptly, so that the basic needs of the
worker and those dependent upon her may be satisfied.

Yet in the context of the time allotted to every human
being, the requirement takes on an added dimension. If the
employer delays payment, the worker's time is inevitably devalued
and wasted. If he is a regular employee, he learns that his life is
unfairly manipulated to profit another. Even if he is a day laborer
who will never work for the same employer again, he must return
to the place of work, track down the employer, and reissue his
demand. Whether he successfully procures his pay or not, he has
unnecessarily expended time that could have been invested in
the search for more employment, in actual work, family commit-
ments, or even leisure. Indeed, withholding his wage is an act
of moral arrogance as well as deceit. This is precisely what Rav
Hisda identified as "oppression."

The underlying protest against the assumption of one
man's power over the time of another resonates in the Sages'
exchange over the point at which payment becomes due. They
defend the rights and value of the lowliest day worker when they
speak of laborers "engaged by the hour":

(Mishnah): If engaged by the hour, he can collect
it all day and night. (Gemara): Rav said: "A man
engaged by the hour for day work can collect

all day; for night work, he can collect all night."
Samuel maintained: "A man engaged by the hour
for day work can collect it all day; for night work,
all night and the following day." (BT Bava Metzia
111a)

The common sense of the law was so self-evident that the
Sages agreed that workers should not be humbled by the need to
even request their pay:

Our Rabbis taught: The wages of him that is hired
shall not abide all night. I might think this holds
good even if he did not demand it. (BT Bava
Metzia 112a)

Although the Sages agreed that a worker's time must
be compensated if work had been promised and then retracted,
they struggled with the particulars—how much, and under what
conditions. Should the laborer be fully compensated for his time,
or only partially, since he was then free to find other work or
engage in some other activity? The tradition teaches that the
employer's burden varies with his level of responsibility for the
situation:

(Mishnah): If the employer retracts, he is at a
disadvantage. He who alters (the contract) is at a
disadvantage, and he who retracts is at a disadvantage. (BT Bava Metzia 76a) . . . (Gemara): (H)e
must pay them in full. Yet travelling with a load
is not the same as travelling empty-handed, nor

is working the same as sitting idle ... If they have commenced work, the portion done is assessed for them. (BT Bava Metzia 76b)

If an employer simply cancels work, he is liable for the employee's loss. But since the worker's time opens up for other opportunities, the employer need not pay at the full wage level since "travelling with a load is not the same as travelling empty-handed." However, if work has been performed and then abruptly cancelled, the calculation must involve payment for work done and then, in addition, assessment of promised time lost, perhaps on a different scale of compensation.

Nor can an employer arbitrarily substitute other work that shortchanges employees. He may keep them busy with work of the same or a lesser level of difficulty. But if a new task is more difficult, "he cannot order them to do it and must pay them in full."

> Rava also said: If one engaged laborers for a piece of work, and they completed it in the middle of the day; if he has some (other) work easier than the first, he can give it to them, or even if of equal difficulty, he can charge them (with it); but if it is more difficult, he cannot order them to do it, and must pay them in full. (BT Bava Metzia 77a)

What is meant by "pay them in full"? As we'll see shortly, more difficult work warrants higher wages. Given the tenor of Rava's comment, it seems reasonable to conclude that if employees accept the more difficult task, then, "pay them in full" refers to the normal rate for that sort of job, which is likely higher than the less difficult task they had already completed.

Quite often—in modern work environments as well as in ancient ones—work is cancelled due to conditions beyond the control of either employer or employee:

> If one engaged laborers to cut dykes, and rain fell and rendered (the land) waterlogged (making work impossible), if (the employer) inspected it the previous evening, the loss is the workers; if not, the loss is the employer's, and he must pay them as unemployed workers. (BT Bava Metzia 76b–77a)

If the employer performs due diligence, assures that conditions are adequate to cut the dykes, and notifies his employees in good faith that everything is ready for work, then his technical liability is mitigated if conditions suddenly change (though, as other cases indicate, an ethical obligation remains).[97] But if he has not checked the conditions, then he must pay them at least "as unemployed workers;" that is, at the level of someone still seeking employment, presumably the minimum rate that local practice established for that job. The same logic holds true for other natural occurrences as long as the workers are clearly informed of a situation or should otherwise know not to show up—a "reasonable man" standard. But if the workers could not have reasonably known that conditions made work impossible, they still must be paid—as in this case of a river that overflows and randomly irrigates the cropland around it. Unlike the employer, workers are not required to proactively inspect the field before punching in:

Rava also said: "If one engaged laborers for irrigation, and there fell rain (rendering it unnecessary), the loss is theirs. But if the river overflowed, the loss is the employer's, and he must pay them as unemployed laborers." (BT Bava Metzia 77a)

Just as unforeseeable events might cause the cancellation of work and reduce the employer's liabilities at the expense of the employee, so natural and life cycle events that cause employees to leave a job early or miss it altogether do not excuse the employer from compensating them for work performed:

Has it not been taught: If one engages a laborer, and in the middle of the day, he (the laborer) learns that he has suffered a bereavement, or is smitten with fever, then if he is a time worker, (the employer) must pay him his wages; if a contract worker, he must pay him his contract price. (BT Bava Metzia 77a)

The Sages go on to note that even if the worker's decision to leave is questionable, the employer's responsibility to compensate him is not diminished; neither wage nor contract workers can be penalized for retracting the labor agreement:

Even if the employee is not compelled (to break the agreement), surely the Rabbis maintain that the laborer has the advantage. (BT Bava Metzia 77b)

The traditional Jewish perspective looks at the employee as a whole person, not a product, and protects her rights accordingly.

Spoken and Implicit Arrangements

Employers are tempted, especially during stressful periods in the economic cycle, to unilaterally alter the rules of the workplace to their own advantage. The opposition of the Ancients to unilateral changes in the workplace suggests a social contract that would today protect unionized and unaffiliated workers alike:

> (Mishnah): One who engages laborers and demands that they commence early or work late—where local usage is not to commence early or work late he may not compel them. Where it is the practice to supply food (to laborers), he must supply them; even to provide a relish, he must provide it. Everything depends on local custom . . . (Gemara): Is it not obvious? It is necessary (to teach this) only when (the employer) pays them a higher wage (than usual). He can plead, "I pay you a higher wage in order that you may start earlier and work for me until nightfall"; But we are taught that they can reply, "The higher pay is for better work (not longer hours)." (BT Bava Metzia 83a)

What the Sages reference here as "local custom" is immediately recognizable to employees in a vast array of industrial and service settings as "past practice." In the often harsh cycle of physical work, employees rely on known routines for comfort and respite. Sudden disruptions of those routines—tightened rules for breaks, requirements to report trips to the bathroom, forced overtime or weekend work, increased production demands—all infringe on the *de facto* social contract that governs every place of work, from production lines to call centers and nursing homes. When a contract is broken—when, in the words of the Sages, a party retracts or is deceived—then the fragile symbiosis between employer and employee frays, frequently with injury to all sides. Time, production, profit—and sometimes jobs and prosperity— are lost:

> If one hires laborers and they deceive the employer,
> or the employer deceives them, they have nothing
> but resentment against each other (but no legal
> redress). (BT Bava Metzia 76b)

It is precisely employee resentment over broken practices—from comfort breaks to the abrupt introduction of new technologies—that disrupt the precarious balance of the workplace. Understanding this dynamic, the Ancients outlined contingent solutions that bear a striking resemblance to modern contractual remedies. But, like modern minimum wage laws, theirs is a social contract, not a private one, covering all employees without respect to bargaining agreements.

Whether speaking of a labor-management agreement or, as in this instance, a commercial transaction, the ethic of the Just Market is the same; the party who breaks a contract, or attempts to change its terms mid-course, is not only in the wrong but subject to penalties that leave him with the worst of the deal:

If the purchaser retracts, the vendor has the advantage . . . (the vendor) can say to him, "Here is your money." Alternatively, he can say, "Here is land for your money." And what (part of the field) may he offer (the purchaser)? The worst. (BT Bava Metzia 77b)

Apply this example to the labor relations scenario that surrounds it in the source text. An employer who breaks a deal with employees (including unilateral changes in past practices) should expect "the worst part" in return—grudging labor, sluggishly performed—or even refusal to work. And against that response from employees, there would be no redress.

Just Compensation

The Sages were wary of an exchanged product that would not be as useful to workers as cash, and of employers who might reduce compensation levels by offering product that had dropped in price, cheating employees who were unlikely to be on top of market fluctuations. Employers were therefore required to pay wages in negotiable currency. The prohibition also blocks company store arrangements in which the assessed cost of a provided product is determined by the employer and billed against the worker's fixed wage. In today's economy, this prohibition is particularly applicable to the situation of modern indentures—undocumented workers (discussed further in the next chapter) whose conditions of labor too often include deductions for mandatory housing and supplies:

> If a man engages a laborer to work for him on
> straw . . . and when he demands his wages, says to
> him, take the results of your labor for your wage,
> he is not heeded. (BT Bava Metzia 118a)

In the Talmudic epoch, the most common non-wage
benefit seems to have been food on the job. In virtually all cases,
providing meals was an employer obligation, not an option. The
nature of the meal itself, even to the dessert, was mandatory per
local custom, along with unlimited snacking on crops. Payment
was fixed in advance, and benefits like meals and snacks were
added on top.

At their option, employees—and only employees—could
elect to forego benefits in order to increase cash compensation.
In this case, the head of a working family required that the entire
family's benefits be added as cash to their wages. He is permitted
to speak for the family because all are "of age"—that is, old enough
to understand the trade-off:

> A man may stipulate to receive payment instead
> of eating for himself, his son or daughter that are
> of age, his manservant and maidservant that are
> of age, and his wife; because they have under-
> standing. (BT Bava Metzia 92b)

Similarly, the Sages prohibited employers from setting
up "partnerships" in which workers sacrificed some or all of their
fixed pay for the possibility of shared profit in the employer's
project or enterprise. Nothing stopped employees from using
savings or other existing assets to invest in their employer's busi-

ness (an apparently rare occurrence at that time). But the deferral of wages to do so is prohibited, freeing employees from pressures to assume the risk of either their employer's enterprise or his accounting procedures. Here employers are enjoined from enticing workers with a share of profits in lieu of wage compensation:

> A man may not commission a tradesman on a half profit basis nor advance money for provisions to be sold on half profits, unless he pays him a wage as a worker. Fowls may not be set to brood on half profits nor may calves or foals be assessed in that way, unless he pays him for his labor and foodstuffs. (BT Bava Metzia 68a)

The right to bundle all forms of compensation as cash maximized the employee's flexibility. He could spend as he needed, perhaps invest in tools, or even save to buy a shop necessary to advance a rung on the competitive ladder.

A Minimum Wage

The Sages expected that employers would naturally attempt to minimize their labor costs. And while the tradition recognizes the need for wage flexibility, there are limits.

Commenting on the efficacy of paying a wage in advance to hedge against rising labor costs, Rava might be interpreted to argue rhetorically against a wage floor itself:

What a logical argument! Has it ever been forbidden to reduce one's hire to the lowest level? (BT Bava Batra 87a)

Yet in the context of his other commentaries, it is obvious that Rava is sympathetic to the hardship caused by low wages. Nor is he averse to mitigating their impact on the poorest workers. For example, he notes that minimum wages must be protected, even for those who transgress the quite serious laws of the Sabbatical Year:

> Rava . . . said: (T)he difficulty you raise over the teaching concerning the workman (who gathers fruits in the Sabbatical Year) can be met by the answer that in the case of a laborer whose wage is small the Rabbis did not impose a penalty. (BT Avodah Zarah 62b)

Through this lens, Rava aligns with the dominant view of the Ancients. They not only refer to a bottom-level wage, but explicitly reject it as too low if a new worker is hired:

> If one engages a laborer, and stipulates, "(I will pay you) as one or two townspeople (are paid)," he must remunerate him with the lowest wage (paid). This is Rav Yehoshua's view. But the Sages say: An average must be struck. (BT Bava Metzia 87a)

And so, a more definitive sense of wage compensation emerges. Rav Yehoshua posits that a laborer must be paid the minimum wage in effect in his market—not a newly established, even lower wage, no matter how desperate for work the laborer might be. But his view is soundly rejected by the majority, which specifies that the employee must receive the average wage then prevailing for the type of work in question—and not merely the minimum wage then in effect. In practice, this procedure results in a steady minimum wage increase over time.

We can assume from the Ancients' determination to promote universal access to the necessities of life that an acceptable wage level would satisfy the needs of a worker and his or her family. Economist Lawrence Glickman expresses what might be considered a contemporary version of their outlook by describing a "living wage" as

> . . . a wage level that offers workers the ability to support families, to maintain self-respect, and to have both the means and the leisure to participate in the civic life of the nation.[98]

What does this mean in the contemporary economy? We might assume that the official poverty line, plus social entitlements triggered by that level of income, represent the minimum amount required to access the necessities of life—by even the most conservative definition. For example, a poverty line multiple of 130% falls within the recognized needs bracket for food stamps. For a typical family of three, then, the ability to access even basic food necessities must be at least 130% of the poverty line plus the value of food stamps themselves. That works out to about $32,300 per year, which corresponds to a minimum wage of $15.50/hour.[99] We might reasonably conclude that a Just Market scenario requires wages at that level, at least.

Beyond that, Talmudic wage discussions usually compare relative compensation under different conditions (during harvest and non-harvest periods, before work commences or after it is completed, if tasks are finished or abandoned in the middle of the job). Although we do not learn much about absolute pay levels from these Talmudic cases, we can understand relationships of scale of income, which are critical to any modern application.

Thus, we can only guess whether six *denari* is a high wage or a low one, or whether it will sustain a family. But we do learn that the value of a laborer's time differs if he completes his job as promised or not, and what the scale of that difference might be:

> (If) they have commenced work (and then stopped), the portion done is assessed for them. If they contract to harvest standing corn for two *selas* and they harvest half, and leave half; or to weave a garment for two *selas* and they weave half and leave half, the portion done is assessed. If it is worth six *denari*, he must pay them a *sela* (four *denari*). Or they can complete the work and receive two *selas* (full payment). If it is worth a *sela*, he must pay them a *sela*. (BT Bava Metzia 76b)

Another opinion on the matter is then expressed, but the concept of relative wage scales is not challenged. (Curiously, both views agree that if half the work is completed, full payment for that half must be made.) If an employee breaks his agreement and halts work without good reason, he receives only two-thirds of the value of the work that was performed—the "worst of the deal." (As we've seen, an employee's decision to terminate work due to sickness or bereavement is exempt from any wage penalty.)

At another point, the Sages discuss an employer's agent who hires workers. A distinction is drawn between a wage that is considered respectful and one that is not, given the specific nature of the job. Some employees react badly to the discovery that their wage is three zuz while others are paid four zuz for the same job. While the three- and four-zuz wage levels may be purely hypothetical, in the context of the other examples it's likely that the relative scale of wages accurately reflects the Sages' sense of a reasonable wage gap:

> It is necessary (to teach this) only when some engage themselves for four and others for three. (T)hey can say to (the foreman): "Had you not told us that it is for four zuz, we would have taken the trouble to find employment at four." Alternatively, this may refer to a (contractor who) can say to him, "Had you not promised me four, it would have been beneath my dignity to accept employment." (BT Bava Metzia 76a)

The four-zuz payment is not a premium or even an average. Rather, it seems to be at the top of the wage scale for this job. As the Talmudic passage progresses, we discover that conscientious work underlies the difference, even when menial jobs like filling and stacking bags of dirt on a dyke are at issue. In the absence of poor-quality work, the minimum wage is disrespectful, inviting discontent and resistance:

(The employees) can say to (the foreman): "Since
you told us it was for four, we took the trouble of
doing the work particularly well."... This refers to
a dyke. But even in a dyke, it (superior workman-
ship) may be distinguished! (BT Bava Metzia 76a)

In sum, the texts suggest that if an employer offers to pay
only the minimum when he knows that conscientious work will
be performed, he disrupts the social contract that requires the
higher scale. And since "if the employer retracts, he is at a disadvantage," he should expect that his laborers will leave him with
"the worst" of the deal.

Where an employer increases wages and then uses the
higher wage to extract longer hours, the Ancients deny him, reas-
serting that premium pay is rightfully attributed to high-quality
work. We looked at this text earlier as commentary on unilateral changes in working conditions. Now consider its view on the
nature of wages:

When (the employer) pays them a higher wage
(than usual)... (h)e can plead, "I pay you a higher
wage in order that you start earlier and work for
me until nightfall." We are therefore taught that
they can reply, "The higher remuneration is for
better work (but not longer hours)." (BT Bava
Metzia 83a)

So while absolute wage levels are not regulated and
vary with the nature of the work involved, it is only logical that
wages must be in line with the Talmudic objective of providing

universal access to the necessities of life. Moreover, the tradition offers guidelines regarding wage gaps for like tasks. Wages must be offered between a fixed minimum and an average that reflects local practice; the dominant view among the Ancients mandates the higher yardstick, even for new employees. A higher top-level wage should be used to determine the minimum acceptable compensation, which reduces the uppermost pay for a given task by not more than 25% (the difference between four and three zuz). Anything less is "beneath the dignity" of employees. The basis for the difference is the quality or conscientiousness of work, not the economic power of the employer or his preference for greater profits.

Respect for Life, Even on the Job

While examining another issue in chapter 2, we looked at a ruling that prohibited the use of scythes among gleaners, who were untrained and so likely to injure one another in the competition for leftover crops.[100] Remarkable as it may be in an ancient setting, this is no isolated instance of concern about safety on the job.

The employer's responsibility for the safety of his work-force is indicated in the case of the blacksmith who fatally injures an apprentice when the blacksmith's sparks fly from the anvil into the younger man's face:

> Is an apprentice of a smith to be killed without punishment? (Only) where his master had urged him to leave but he did not leave. But even where his master had been urging him to leave, may he be killed without punishment? Only where the

master believed that he had already left. (BT Bava Kamma 32b)

The employer's liability for the deceased worker is precisely the same as it would have been had the blacksmith accidentally killed someone on the street. The Ancients did not recognize any special circumstance, nor offer any veneer of regulatory protection to an employer simply because an accident occurred on the job. This is the diametric opposite of the regulatory "alphabet soup" recalled by federal prosecutor Jonathan Zell that protects "factory owners who ignore safety rules and thereby injure their workers."[101]

The story of the blacksmith's apprentice resonates in the plaintive words of the Sages, which suggest broad employer responsibility for the well-being of a worker who has no choice but to perform under the conditions that are presented to him:

> Why does (the worker) climb a ladder or hang
> from a tree or risk death? Is it not for his wages?
> Another interpretation: "His life depends on
> them." (BT Bava Metzia 112a)

So important is the safety of the laborer on the job—who is intent on "hanging from a tree or risking death" on behalf of wages to feed his family—that even the most central prayer obligations are placed on the back burner in physically risky situations:

> Our Rabbis taught: Workmen may recite (the
> *Sh'ma* prayer) on the top of a tree or on the top of
> a scaffolding, and they may say the *t'filah* (prayer)

on the top of an olive tree and the top of a fig tree,[102] but from all other trees they must come down to the ground before saying the t'filah, and the employer must in any case come down before saying the t'filah, the reason in all cases being that their mind is not clear. (BT Berakhot 16a)

If an owner's sickness or physical condition puts employees at risk, the employer is required to take adequate precautions to protect them:

(Mishnah): (The sick employer) may not eat with him out of a bowl put before workmen, nor may he work with him on the same furrow: This is Rav Meir's view. But the Sages say: "He may work, provided he is at a distance." . . . (Gemara): . . . There is no dispute at all that they may not work near (each other. But) Rav Meir maintains: We forbid at a distance as a preventive measure . . . , while the Rabbis hold: "We do not enact a preventive measure." (BT Nedarim 41b)

The Presumption of Collective Action

In addition to the refusal to work under emotionally fraught or physically dangerous situations, we have already identified examples of collective activity that appear to be accepted and sanctioned as the norm. At Bava Metzia 83a, employees collectively respond to an employer's effort to force longer hours by offering additional compensation: "They can reply, 'The higher remuneration is for better work.'" At Bava Metzia 76a, employees seek to head off a proposed wage cut by responding together: "Since you told us it was for four zuz, we took the trouble of doing the work particularly well." Laborers are depicted jointly demanding wages from a recalcitrant employer in the marketplace at Bava Metzia 46a. The explicit rights of artisans to "establish work shifts amongst themselves" and assume other guild-like powers suggest additional rights of combination,[103] although these resemble modern trade associations as much as unionized or other collective activities.

A vivid example of the legitimacy of collective activity is transmitted by the Talmudic recounting of workers who gather at the home of their employer "to demand their wages from him." (Recall the earlier admonition that a demand for wages should not be needed at all.) The Ancients debate whether the workers' demands are most appropriately put at the owner's office, at his home, or both. They discuss the locus of liability if an employee is injured (bitten by a dog or gored by an ox) while making demands at the employer's residence. There is no question that this text is about collective activity; all references to employees and their actions in the original texts are in the plural. *What is never questioned in the text* is the absolute right of employees to take collective action to assure redress of a grievance—and the apparent normalcy of doing so. All the more astonishing is that this passage was codified when slavery was still common throughout the world's cultures:

> Our Rabbis taught: If employees come to (the private residence of) their employer to demand their wages from him and (it so happens that) their employer's ox gores them or their employer's dog bites them with fatal results, (then) he (the

employer) is exempt. Others, however, maintain that employees have the right to (come and)
demand their wages from their employer (even
at his residence). Now, what were the circumstances? If the employer could be found in (his)
city (offices), what reason (could be adduced) for
(the view maintained by) the "Others"? If (on the
other hand) he could be found only at home, what
reason (could be given) for (the view expressed
by) the first *Tanna*? No, the application (of the
case) is where the employer could (sometimes)
be found (in his offices) but could not (always) be
found (there). The employees therefore called at
his (private) door. (BT Bava Kamma 33a)

All employees not only maintain the right to express griev-
ances, but where necessary, to pursue an elusive employer to his
residence, and resolve their demands. The nature of their action—
whether individual or collective—does not affect that right. We
can presume that if the Ancients recognized those rights, they
also protected those who exercised them from retribution.

People or Products?

The Western concept of the market imbues corporations with the
rights of persons, and assesses the value of individuals as if they
were products. The Just Market rejects both of these concepts.

The Just Market view of labor relations is based on ethical,
respectful behavior between parties to economic transactions,
whether their relationship is that of employer and employee or

parties to business contracts. A business contract, like the social contract, creates a committed bond between parties, each of whom must respect the letter and spirit of an unforced agreement or suffer consequences.

Both laborer and owner have an intrinsic right to the respectful treatment due to every individual in every social situation. The value of human time is equivalent. Unilateral abrogation of contracts or implicit arrangements is prohibited. Compensation levels that ensure access to the necessities of life are required. Safe working conditions are mandatory, even at the inconvenience of business owners. Collective action, whether by formal organizations or spontaneous groups, is respected.

Even those requirements are surpassed by the presumption of doubt that the Ancients passed down as an ethical guide to justice—one that goes beyond the letter of the law—in the labor relationship. Their perspective is encapsulated in the case of laborers who negligently break a barrel of wine belonging to the son of the Sage Rav Huna.

Knowing that these laborers have no cash with which to compensate him, the son seizes their cloaks instead. But another Sage intervenes:

> "Return their garments," Rav ordered. The son of Rav Huna asked, "Is that the law?" "Even if it is not strictly the law," Rav answered, "(Do it anyway) 'that you walk in the way of good men.'" The garments were returned. The laborers said, "We are poor men, have worked all day, and are in need. Are we to get nothing?" "Go and pay them," Rav ordered. "Is that the law?" asked the son of

Rav Huna. "Even if not," Rav replied (citing from
Proverbs 2:20): 'Keep (to) the path of the righteous.'" (BT Bava Metzia 83a)

The modern market reduces employee rights to the legal-
ized formalities of unions and limited government agencies that,
despite successes, are mired in regulatory procedures that deny
meaningful application of Just Market values to hundreds of thousands of employees each year. This is the inevitable result, despite
all good intentions, of channeling issues that are fundamentally
within the purview of a social contract into private contracts and
remote, emasculated regulators.

These are not abstract issues. I've personally known
workers who have been fired—denied access to the necessities of
life—because they refused to work overtime day after exhausting
day, weekend after weekend. I've known employees who were
terminated due to pregnancies; and others who have been killed
or maimed on the job due to employer negligence for which the
perpetrator has gone unpunished and his shell of protection—the
corporation—merely slapped on the wrist.

By contrast, the Just Market offers a different model—
one that recognizes the importance of local practices established
over time, but that also provides a broad umbrella of rulings that
binds workers and employers in all situations, whether individual
or collective, with or without legal recognition. It is a model in
which employers and employees alike are treated as adults personally responsible for their actions; in which demands on a worker's
time cannot be compelled by employers beyond social norms;
and in which the wasted time of even the most humble worker
deserves compensation.

Eighty-three percent of US employees experience chronic work stress, according to a 2013 survey sponsored by Everest College. While 14% ranked poor compensation as the primary stressor at work, 31% cited work overload and employer-generated insecurity and frustration as the primary forms of on-the-job stress that they experience.[104] Respectful practices and a living wage are as important to the personal satisfaction objectives of the Just Market today as they were two thousand years ago.

From Ethics to Advocacy

In an era of increasing individualism and the deterioration of wages and working conditions—first in the vulnerable manufacturing sector and now in growth sectors like retail, services, and health—traditional union affinity has withered. The Just Market establishes protections that recognize basic human and social needs for respect and honest engagement in the labor-management environment. It mandates ethical workplace behavior regardless of bargaining status. Policing mechanisms centered in localized bodies enforce rapid decisions on wages, terminations, violations of implied and written contracts, and safety violations. The Just Market would:

- *Recognize the rights of mutually recognized "past practices" on the job.*

- *Value the time rights of every employee* regarding wages lost due to production flow problems and retracted work; enforce payment on time for work performed by all employees; and for paid time off for life cycle events.

- *Prosecute criminal employer liability* for unsafe conditions and practices.

- *Institute wage standards based on the average level* for that job in the market area; establish a *minimum wage that meaningfully provides access to the necessities of life*; and create a *maximum wage differential standard for like jobs.*

- *Protect the right to collective action* in both unionized and non-union settings; *and to individual action in support of conditions required by Just Market guidelines.*

6. SABBATICAL VALUES

The far-reaching social and economic implications of the Sabbatical Year (*Shmita*) and the Jubilee Year (*Yovel*) have been effectively buried for two thousand years. The Shmita (literally Year of Release) occurs once every seventh year, while the Jubilee, the Sabbatical of Sabbaticals, is marked on each forty-ninth or fiftieth—the chronicles are fuzzy on the precise method of calculation. Both cycles release the impoverished from servitude in various forms and activate escape routes from crushing cycles of debt. The Yovel creates an additional mechanism to promote economic opportunity for successive generations.

The Shmita is discussed several times in the books of Exodus, Leviticus, Deuteronomy, and again in Jeremiah, Nehemiah, 2 Chronicles, and Kings. It is the subject of dozens of references in Talmud. The breadth of these sources suggests the normative nature of ancient sabbatical practices. Evidence of Jubilee Year practice, on the other hand, is not as definitive. Traditional commentators assert that "the Jubilee was observed only as long as the entire territory of the Holy Land was inhabited by Israelites,"[105] since the nature of some Jubilee laws required enforcement by a dominant culture.

Seven objectives are indicated for these two related celebrations in the original texts, including human responsibility for stewardship of the land of Israel and renewed public commitment to study and learn Jewish history and laws. Without minimizing these two elements, our discussion centers on the five market-related values inherent in the original laws: economic renewal, embodied in the year of rest and regeneration of the land; release from intractable poverty cycles through the erasure of debt; freedom from indentured servitude; the refreshment of the apparatus of wealth creation through the sabbatical process; and re-leveling the economic playing field through the transfer of economic assets to successive generations.

In the Judaic tradition, violations of the Shmita and the Yovel are equated to the most despicable of sins. Even the fall of the second Temple and the subsequent two-thousand-year exile of the Jewish people from the land of Israel have been attributed to widespread resistance to the Sabbatical and Jubilee laws.

> As a punishment for . . . non-observance of the years of release and jubilee, exile comes to the world. The Jews are exiled, and others come and dwell in their place . . . "The land is defiled—so do I visit iniquity upon it, that the land vomit you out, when you defile it." (BT Shabbat 33a, quoting from Leviticus 18:25)

And not only humans were penalized. Plant stock or trees that were planted or tended in violation of the Sabbatical Year were also uprooted.

> There must be no planting, no sinking and no grafting on the eve of the Sabbatical Year ... and if one planted or sank or grafted, the tree must be uprooted. (BT Yevamot 83a)

Individual violations of the Shmita triggered a three-part rehabilitation process. Full rehabilitation could only be finalized at the next Shmita, seven years later. The process included a specified period of community ostracism and a requirement to prove genuine repentance in practice. After these social requirements were satisfied, financial penalties (in the amount of the Sabbatical produce traded) still had to be paid as compensation to the poor. Only then was the process complete:

> Sabbatical traders are those who trade in the produce of the Shmita. They cannot be rehabilitated until another Sabbatical Year comes round and they desist from trading. Rav Nehemia said: The Rabbis did not mean a mere verbal repentance, but a reformation that involves monetary reparation. How so? He must declare, "I, so and so, have amassed two hundred zuz by trading in Sabbatical Year produce, and now I give them over to the poor as a gift." (BT Sanhedrin 25b)

The Oral Law classified Shmita violators among the least trustworthy members of society, barring them from civic duties that required honesty and trust.

> And these are ineligible to be witnesses or judges:
> a gambler with dice, a pigeon trainer, and traders
> in the produce of the Sabbatical Year. (BT Sanhe-
> drin 24a)

As we'll see, the Shmita provided unprecedented tools for the renewal of personal hope and the replenishment of society's most critical economic resources. No wonder that violations of Sabbatical Year laws triggered not only severe financial penalties, but also social disgrace.

Release from the Cycle of Debt

The first mention of the Shmita in Deuteronomy calls for release from financial obligations undertaken during the previous seven years.

> Every seventh year you shall practice remission of
> debts . . . (E)very creditor shall remit the due that
> he claims from his neighbor; he shall not dun his
> neighbor or kinsman for the remission. (Deuter-
> onomy 15:1–2)

The source text differentiates between "neighbor" and "kinsman" (the literal translation is "brother"), indicating that the Jewish practice of debt release extended to the gentile community—an interpretation buttressed by multiple discussions in Talmud that presume the side-by-side residential and life proximity of Jews and their gentile neighbors. (Shabbat 82a; Avodah Zarah 26b, for example).

In ancient times, the beneficiary of a loan was most commonly a subsistence farmer struggling through periods between harvests—that is, a family business. From the farmer's perspective, the objective of the loan was to stabilize and rescue the weakest of agricultural "businesses"; those that could barely carry over from harvest to harvest due to severely stressed cash flows.

The ethic of interest-free lending met with increasing resistance as the Shmita neared. Lenders were warned against the tendency to withhold loans as the Sabbatical Year approached:

> Beware lest you harbor the base thought: "The seventh year, the year of remission, is approaching," so that you are mean to your needy kinsman and give him nothing . . . Give to him readily and have no regrets when you do so. (Deuteronomy 15:9–10)

The reluctance to lend money as the Year of Release approached shut off a lifeline to the great mass of subsistence farmers. The debt release law that had been originally designed to help the poor had instead morphed into an obstacle to the ability of small farmers and others to survive between harvests. In response, Rabbi Hillel the Elder (about 60 BCE–10 CE) proposed a compromise known as the *Prosbul*, which effectively escrowed the debt with a court during the Shmita year. This workaround satisfied the letter of the law that barred an individual from exacting payment of a debt during the Sabbatical and erased the need to resolve the complicated issues of Shmita loan forgiveness. The right to collect debts was effectively reinstated in order to encourage reluctant lenders to continue making interest-free loans, mainly to cash-strapped farmers in the period leading up to the Shmita. Yet the Prosbul failed to provide an adequate compensatory mechanism that responded to the original social basis of debt release. It left intact the core problem of cyclical debt among a population living permanently on the financial precipice.

The rabbis of the Talmud signed on to the Prosbul, but not without qualms:

> A Prosbul prevents the remission of debts (in the Sabbatical Year). This is one of the regulations made by Hillel the Elder. He saw that people were unwilling to lend money to one another and disregarded the precept laid down in the Torah . . . But is it possible that, where according to the Torah the seventh year releases (debt), Hillel should ordain that it should not release? Abaye said: He was dealing with the Sabbatical Year in our time. (BT Gittin 36a)

Abaye's comment at the end of the passage confirms that even ordained law had to be considered in the context of both the historical epoch and its immediate ramifications on the lives of the people and community.

Whether wise or misguided, the Prosbul represented an electrifying step in the development of Jewish law. A direct Torah commandment—not an interpretation, but a direct commandment that was repeated several times—was countermanded by the Sages because it was not working as intended. Basing their acceptance on a threadbare technicality, the Ancients essentially declared that unforeseen consequences (in this case, the inability to access no-interest survival loans, rather than liberation from debt) trumped the divine.

The Prosbul has remained a fixture of halakhic law ever since. Yet the Talmud suggests that the workaround was not intended to be a permanent aspect of Jewish life, but rather, a tool whose deployment depended on historical context and the power of opinion makers at any given point in time.

> When Hillel instituted the Prosbul, did he insti-
> tute it for his own generation only or for future
> generations also? . . . If you say that Hillel insti-
> tuted the Prosbul only for his own generation,
> then we may abolish it, but if for future genera-
> tions also (this would not be easy), since one *beyt
> din* (religious court) cannot annul the decisions
> of another unless it surpasses it in wisdom and in
> numbers . . .
>
> Samuel said . . . if I am ever in a position, I will
> abolish it.
>
> Abolish it? How so, seeing that one beyt din
> cannot annul the decision of another unless it is
> superior to it in wisdom and numbers? What he
> meant was: If ever I am in a stronger position than
> Hillel, I will abolish it. Rav Nakhman, however,
> said: I would confirm it. (BT Gittin, 36b)

Based on the commentaries passed down by the tradition, practices around debt release could change again as social needs and the consequences of existing practice evolve—and certainly if the context of events suggested a return to practices more in line with original Torah law.

Real life forced the Ancients to mitigate the cyclical release of debt. In the modern economy, the concern of the earlier epoch—a lack of lenders—simply doesn't exist. But crushing debt cycles that result from an inability to access the necessities of life, or from the heavily promoted lures of materialist culture, are still with us.

By May 2012, 31.4% of all US mortgage borrowers were "underwater"—owing more on their homes than they were worth. Almost four years after the recession hit, the percentage of underwater loans was down only slightly more than a single point from 2011. As we now know, the blame rests most heavily with mortgage and investment bankers who increased subprime loans tenfold in ten years—from $65 billion in 1995 to $665 billion in 2005—and then bet against their own loans in the hedge fund market. When those loans began to fail, the real estate market was flooded and prices plummeted.[106] (A similar crisis is predicted by the central Bank of Israel. A bank-sponsored study concluded in 2013 that 17% of all Israeli mortgages rely on payments that require at least 40% of the mortgagee's household income, reflecting a housing bubble that has seen home prices jump 54% between 2008 and 2012, while wages increased by only 20% over the same period. In September 2013, the Bank of Israel stopped approving mortgages that called for monthly payments of more than half of mortgagee income.)[107]

Nor is the US mortgage scandal the only reflection of a debt crisis. As far back as 2001, household debt had begun to exceed household income, effectively throwing the average US family into the red. After peaking in 2007, household debt was still at 120% of income by 2011.[108]

One long-term culprit is a financial environment that encourages predatory credit card and payday lending. As of May 2011, credit card debt was a staggering $15,956 per US household, accounting for a substantial portion of the average debt-to-income ratio.[109] Credit card delinquency rates ranged from over 3.6% to more than 9% in the decade 2001–2011 (table 6-1), suggesting that somewhere in between lay the percentage of cyclically burdened debtors among the nation's 180 million credit card holders. (With the burden of the latest recession beginning to ease, both delinquency and charge-off rates fell in 2012.)

Table 6-1. Credit Card Delinquency and Charge-offs

	Delinquency (%)	Charge-Offs (%)
2001	4.86	5.42
2002	4.87	6.42
2003	4.47	5.84
2004	4.11	5.04
2005	3.70	4.84
2006	4.01	3.64
2007	4.25	4.00
2008	5.02	5.52
2009	6.52	9.40
2010	4.90	9.35
2011	3.54	5.68
2012	2.72	4.07

Source: Federal Reserve

Since 2010, the incidence of those caught in the cyclical debt cycle has ranged as high as 10.2 million. The delinquency rate is bolstered by state laws that limit maximum interest rates of 5% to 12% for "normal" lending purposes but place no controls on credit card rates (or on interstate banking, which is regulated by the federal government). Stiglitz calls it "a credit and debit card system that not only exploits consumers but imposes large fees on merchants," thereby driving up costs for everyone except merchant banks. On top of misleading bankruptcy reforms "designed to allow (banks) to make bad loans to people who didn't understand what was going on," this adds up to what he terms "the new indentured servitude law."[110]

While in the Talmudic era a lack of available credit was the most common cause of spiraling debt foreclosure, property loss, and even personal freedom, today it is the casual, convenient availability of credit that lures people from sound fiscal practices into a spiral of debt. Aside from credit cards, easy money schemes offered by the payday check-cashing industry and pawn shops entice economically disadvantaged populations through a variation of g'nivat da'at (stealing the mind) that promises easy credit or cash availability at (often obscured) exorbitant rates, plus bank fees. Proliferating in urban areas, these have become a $30 billion–plus industry with more than thirty thousand US outlets.[111]

A modern version of Shmita debt release would be based on a seven-year cycle of *Shmita Credit Forgiveness* for credit card- and payday-related debt. Faced with an approaching debt release deadline, both credit card and payday industries will become increasingly reluctant to issue high-risk credit, reducing the burden of the debt cycle for the population for several years before the Shmita year itself. At the seventh year, remaining debt is erased.

Noting the Ancients' assumption of loans for basic needs at zero interest, a Just Market ethic would also cap interest rates for credit card, banking, and payday loans at the existing maximum interest rates permitted for all other business and personal loans in the state of the consumer.

Release from Servitude

If a farmer in the biblical epoch lost his footing, he could not repay even the traditional interest-free debt. His predicament was likely to result in either indentured servitude or the forced sharecropping decried in Isaiah's plaint against landlords who "join field to field" (Isaiah 5:8). The Shmita and Jubilee laws proclaiming release from indentured servitude provided an escape hatch from this gruesome cycle.

> "If a fellow Hebrew, man or woman, is sold to you,
> he shall serve you six years, and in the seventh year
> you shall set him free." (Deuteronomy 15:12)

The rabbinic understanding is that the prescribed seven-year cycle for release of indentured servants is during the Shmita year, not the seventh year of servitude itself.[112] The entire basis of indenture was the debt that forced a bondsman to sell himself to pay off his obligation in lieu of wages. If the Shmita cancelled the debt, then the basis for indenture dissolved.

Isador Grunfeld, a former judge of the London beyt bin, concludes that the full triad of release mechanisms was activated in the Shmita year:

> During the seventh year the land must lie fallow
> . . . A Hebrew man or a Hebrew woman who has

been sold for service to a fellow Jew, is to be set
free in the seventh year. At the end of the seventh
year, debts are to be annulled so that a creditor is
legally barred from collecting the money owing to
him.[113]

But what happened when the Prosbul disrupted the practice of debt release? Did the temporary conveyance of debt to a
court also mean that any related indenture was continued during
and after the Shmita? In other words, did the Prosbul compromise also cancel the right of an indentured servant to liberty in
the seventh year?

Since the Torah requirement to free indentured servants
is stated independent of the command to release debt, it seems
unlikely that the Prosbul (which does not address indenture at
all) could also cancel the freedom right of indentured servants by
implication alone. In light of human development over the last
two thousand years, this is a reading that most moderns would no
doubt prefer to adopt.

It's a fact, though, that ancient Jewish law, from Torah
through the period of the Sages, accepted indentured servitude as
a valid if distasteful economic instrument. It's not a happy page
in Jewish civilization, but it's a real one. It would be convenient to
ignore that history. But if we do, we lose the opportunity to learn
how good people tried to mitigate injustice within a tribal world
that often demarcated a dominant population through isolation
of the Other.

Historically, the institution of indentured servitude arose
where people became enmeshed in intractable debt by economic
conditions over which they had no personal control. They surren-

dered their own liberty (and sometimes severed personal relationships) so that family members could maintain a semblance of economic stability. Prodded by the black hand of the market, some initially entered into voluntary arrangements to avoid other penalties they considered more onerous—losing an ancestral land grant, for example.

The Jewish version of indentured servitude was tame compared to common practices of the time—but it was bondage nonetheless. In isolated cases, other societies had technically abolished indentured servitude by the time the Talmud was codified—at least, as in Athens and Rome, for limited populations of freemen and citizens. But those societies retained very common slavery practices. Where indentured servitude *was* practiced outside of Jewish communities, it was without time limits. Under ancient Jewish law, by contrast, the period of allowable indenture was circumscribed.

Jewish society considered indenture an unfortunate and purely financial arrangement governed by rules and social mores. Unlike debtors' prisons that later emerged in Christian Europe, debt in Jewish society was not criminalized. Among Jews, servitude was not an arrangement in which an individual surrendered all rights.

Jewish law included protections, benefits, and a level of respect for indentured servants unheard of in other ancient societies. The period of indenture was seen as a difficult necessity for an individual who needed to create a return path to a better place in the community:

> If your brother under you continues in straits and
> must give himself over to you, do not subject him to

the treatment of a slave. He shall remain under you as a hired or bound laborer. (Leviticus 25:39–40)

At the conclusion of the indenture period—whatever its length—masters were under strict obligation to provide the servant a leg up to economic self-reliance. Torah required each master to outfit the liberated bondsman with food and the means to create a livelihood:

When you set him free, do not let him go empty-handed. Furnish him out of the flock, threshing floor, and vat. (Deuteronomy 15:13–14)

While the modern economy has all but eradicated the formal structure of indentured servitude, entrapment in cycles of poverty remain. Its current victims are caught in webs of dictated wages, dead-end jobs, and take-it-or-leave-it conditions. In the most striking parallel to ancient forms of indentured servitude, undocumented workers and sex slaves often suffer living arrangements inspired by the company store model, living under the omnipresent threat of being reported as troublemakers to authorities and sometimes subjected to physical abuse. In 2013, fourteen 7-Eleven stores in the New York area "took in more than $180 million by running a modern-day plantation system" including slave labor practices, according to court documents.[114] In the worst cases, workers in similar situations "owe" transport, job placement, or boarding fees to their "masters," upon whom they ironically depend for survival and protection—directly violating the Just Market prohibition on forcing in-kind compensation on workers (chapter 5).

More of us than want to let on have witnessed the conditions endured by undocumented workers. Two grim images stick with me: scores of African workers languishing in a dusty, decrepit park outside the Tel Aviv bus station, waiting for the hope of a menial job; and my daughter's former coworkers at an upscale restaurant in Harrisburg, PA, condemned to board in a warehouse behind the eatery upon which they depended for a living. The jovial owner deducted mandatory rent from their minimal paychecks, but the workers begged my daughter not to complain to the authorities for fear of losing both their livelihood and their sanctuary.

These are not isolated experiences. A study of immigrant workers in Chicago revealed that undocumented Latin-American men and women experience significantly lower wages (22% and 36% respectively), even where US work experience, education, English proficiency, and occupation are equal to documented workers. In addition:

> Undocumented immigrants report working in unsafe conditions at considerably higher rates relative to immigrants with legal status. Moreover, immigrants without legal status also report alleged wage and hour violations at considerably higher rates relative to documented workers.[115]

Supporting the Chicago study and others similar to it, a Southern Poverty Law Center (SPLC) survey found that "Forty-one percent of those (undocumented workers) surveyed had experienced wage theft where they were not paid for work performed. In New Orleans, an astonishing 80 percent reported wage theft."[116]

The SPLC survey and a series of unrelated newspaper exposés also reveal that undocumented workers are subjected to conditions considered far too dangerous for citizens:

> Overall, 32 percent of Latinos surveyed reported on-the-job injuries. Among those injured on the job, only 37 percent reported that they received appropriate treatment. The remainder of the Latinos who said they suffered on-the-job injuries reported that they were not paid for their lost wages, they did not receive medical care and/or they were fired because they were injured.[117]

Conditions of the estimated 150,000 undocumented workers in Israel (mainly from the former Soviet Union, Africa, and Asia) are similar. Jobs are concentrated in

> . . . workshops, restaurant and cleaning and other domestic services . . . Undocumented workers are helpless and forced to rely upon their employers' sense of fairness . . . Illegal workers have no recourse in cases of exploitation, delinquent wage payment, or inferior working conditions.[118]

The Sabbatical values of the Just Market recognize the effective servitude of undocumented workers and their claim to a level playing field in the seventh year celebration of opportunity. A *Shmita Call for Release* reflects the Jewish ethos of "one law for all," as well as liberty from modern forms of servitude in the seventh year. The Call for Release advocates issuing valid documentation and labor rights to non-seditious, noncriminal undocumented workers every Sabbatical Year.

The calendar of the next biblical Year of Release commences with the holiday of Sukkot in October 2014. The traditional outdoor booths (*sukkot*) erected for the holiday are a reminder of our ancestors' desert journey to liberation from the land of slavery. Especially in the year of the Shmita, there should be room in each *sukkah* for the indentured servants of modernity as well, advocating for the call of Leviticus 19:34 to treat "the stranger who resides with you . . . as one of your citizens."

The Economic Sabbatical

Every seven years, Jews of the First and Second Commonwealth periods (intermittently from about 1000 BCE to 70 CE) engaged in the economic and social cycle of the Shmita. In the original Torah text, the policy of letting the land lie fallow, read literally, is territorially based. As a result, halakhic law historically excluded much of the Shmita from practice outside the land of ancient Israel.[119]

During both the Shmita and the Jubilee Year, farming was prohibited, refreshing society's central economic asset, cultivatable land. The text of the original commandment for the Yovel is quite similar to this passage describing the agricultural restrictions of the Sabbatical Year:

> . . . the land shall observe a sabbath . . . Six years
> you may sow your field and six years you may
> prune your vineyard and gather in the yield. But
> in the seventh year the land shall have a sabbath

of complete rest ... you shall not sow your field or
prune your vineyard. You shall not reap the after-
growth of your harvest or gather the grapes of
your untrimmed vines. (Leviticus 25:2–5)

For the duration of the Shmita, all social strata were
equipped with the same means of survival from the publicly
shared natural produce of the fields:

Six years you shall sow your land and gather in its
yield; but in the seventh you shall let it rest and
lie fallow ... let the needy among your people eat
of it, and what they leave let the wild beasts eat.
(Exodus 23:10–11)

It's one thing to give the land a respite from cultivation
and quite another to surrender the bounty of private property to
the public domain. But farmers large and small were required to
release the naturally occurring produce of their fields and vineyards (*shevi'it*) to the public. Those wealthy enough to possess
fenced land were even required to prop open their gates to facilitate public access to a personal portion of the shevi'it.

Public access to the fields caused practical problems.
Oversight was difficult and some people grabbed more than they
needed. In response, the Ancients stipulated that harvesters could
only take enough to feed themselves and their families.

A procedure called *bi'ur* allowed harvesters to store naturally occurring produce as long as some also remained in the
fields for wild animals. Once the natural supply in the fields was
exhausted, storage was prohibited. To look at it another way, the

more that was left in the fields for slower harvesters and animals, the longer the harvested produce could be stored. This mechanism encouraged balance between the needs of those who stored and those who gleaned day-to-day; and between man and other living things.

During the period of shevi'it harvest, farmers were permitted to stack the natural produce outside their gates, where it was protected as publicly owned (*hefker*). Individuals and families could claim a personal portion of the shevi'it from any farm location.

Eventually, an institution known as the *otzer beyt din* (judicial treasury or storehouse) was developed to oversee the storage of natural produce. The otzer used communal storage facilities to govern distribution to the public. Nominal payment was made to the otzer administration—but only for services rendered in the harvest. Payment based on the value of the natural produce itself was prohibited.

In addition to availing themselves of the publicly accessible produce that grew naturally during the Shmita and Yovel, members of the ancient community were expected to prepare appropriately for the oncoming period of hardship. Despite the wall of laws designed to discourage commercial hoarding (see chapter 1), storage for personal consumption during the Shmita year was expressly permitted in three specific periods: during the Shmita year itself, in the year before, and in the year immediately after the end of the cycle. In keeping with Jewish law, which places saving a life above other commandments, the Sages outlined an alternate scenario in the case of disaster:

Rav said . . . In Palestine one may store fruit (in any of these) three years: The eve of the Sabbatical Year, the Sabbatical Year, and the conclusion of the Sabbatical Year. (But in) years of famine one must not hoard even a *kav* of carobs, because thereby one brings a curse on the market prices. (BT Bava Batra 90b)

The Ancients demarcated clear lines between permitted and prohibited agricultural activities during the Shmita year. The protection of preexisting plant and field stock was approved, while anything that smacked of cultivation or that was designed to improve the productive capabilities of a standing plant (as opposed to sustaining its health) was barred:

Rav Joseph ben Abba said: Rabbah ben Yirmiyahu brought with him this teaching: We may remove worms [from a tree] and patch the bark with dung during the Sabbatical Year . . . we may smear oil on the place of pruning . . . Rabina said: What is the distinction? . . . (I)s patching the bark, the purpose of which is the preservation of the tree and is permitted, analogous to smearing the place of pruning, the purpose of which is to strengthen the tree and is prohibited? . . . According to the view of Rav Ukba ben Hama: There are two ways to work with (olive trees); one to strengthen the tree and this is prohibited and the other to close up cracks and this is permitted. Similarly, there are two kinds of patching; one is to preserve the tree and is permitted and the other to strengthen the tree and is prohibited. (Avodah Zarah 50b)

Likewise, the Ancients warned against efforts to re-enter the production cycle precipitously. Root out the thorns with your extra time, they tell us, but don't rush ahead to create new growth for its own sake. Prevent damage to your assets, but don't expect that you can shortcut the process and still reap its full benefit:

> If a field has been cleared of thorns in the seventh year it can be sown on the expiration of the seventh year. If it has been manured or if cattle have been turned out in order to manure there in the seventh year, it must not be sown at the expiration of the seventh year. (BT Gittin 44a)

Agriculture was the economic engine of ancient society. When crops could not be grown, farm animals and related products that were dependent on agricultural abundance also suffered. Since the economy's driving sector shut down production, money for crafts, trade, and other goods dried up as well. These impacts would have been obvious to the Ancients, who did not spend time iterating them in the texts. When the Just Market considers application of Shmita values to the modern world, the focus goes beyond agriculture to take in the most critical and integrated contemporary economic sectors—the modern equivalents of the ancient agricultural engine.

Yossi Tsuria, a former Executive Vice President for Strategy at NDS, one of Israel's largest technology firms, has written extensively on social and cultural renewal of the Shmita.[120]

He notes that "in the ancient days more than 90 percent of the population of the world worked in agriculture," suggesting that the high-tech sector and other modern economic engines should take on a central role in a revitalized Shmita scenario.[121]

> (In developing modern Shmita procedures) apply the notion of the once-private (agricultural) fields made public. In software, high-tech companies level the playing field by selling their product at cost for the duration of the year. High-tech executives are given time off . . . from their work so that they can refresh themselves spiritually.[122]

In the ancient epoch, the Shmita emphasized stewardship over the land in the service of the divinity. But its practical effect was to give respite to the driving apparatus of wealth production—agriculture—for an entire year.

The modern economy renders specific ancient mechanisms like the harvest of shevi'it unworkable. But society's ability to support the refreshment of its most valuable contemporary resource—labor knowledge—remains.

Based on the Just Market value of refreshing the apparatus of wealth creation, a more limited modern *Shmita Set-Aside* might guarantee a three-month sabbatical to all workers every seven years. Common practice already accepts sabbaticals for specific professions such as college faculty and clerics. Certainly the needs of other employees in an increasingly stressed work environment are no different. Catherine Dunkin, CEO of Standing Partnership, a St. Louis, Missouri–based public relations firm that has pioneered sabbaticals for its twenty-six employees, says that the practice "is one of the greatest retention tools we have."[123]

Table 6-2. Sh'mita Set-Aside Cost as a Per Cent of Sales

	Employee Compensation		Sh'mita Set-Aside Basis	
	IRS	Census	IRS	Census
Agriculture	16.12%	n/a	0.67%	n/a
Mining	14.75%	11.79%	0.61%	0.49%
Utilities	6.99%	10.59%	0.29%	0.44%
Construction	22.23%	21.01%	0.93%	0.88%
Manufacturing	13.77%	13.51%	0.57%	0.56%
Wholesale Trade	7.08%	6.36%	0.29%	0.26%
Retail Trade	11.02%	10.29%	0.46%	0.43%
Transport-Warehousing	29.18%	30.11%	1.22%	1.25%
Information	28.14%	23.74%	1.17%	0.99%
Finance-Insurance	16.43%	15.59%	0.68%	0.65%
Real Estate Rental-Leasing	40.13%	20.21%	1.67%	0.84%
Professional Services	50.10%	41.17%	2.09%	1.72%
Management of Companies	19.65%	n/a	0.82%	n/a
Administrative-Support-Waste Mgt.	67.52%	48.38%	2.81%	2.02%
Educational Services	52.06%	33.46%	2.17%	1.39%
Health Care-Social Assistance	59.77%	43.62%	2.49%	1.82%
Arts-Entertainment-Recreation	30.42%	32.50%	1.27%	1.35%
Accommodation-Food Services	41.24%	29.85%	1.72%	1.24%
Other Services	36.64%	25.61%	1.53%	1.07%

Internal Revenue Service Tax Stats; US Census Bureau 2007 Economic Census

The Shmita Set-Aside would be funded year by year for six years through a company allocation equal to 4.12% (1/24) of total employee compensation to the Fund. The allocation provides for a projected three-month reduction in productive capacity without injuring the economic life of employees. Table 6-2 displays the projected average annual contribution, as a percentage of net sales for each economic sector. (Actual contributions would vary by company.) One-person sole proprietorships would be exempted from the Shmita Set-Aside.

Every employee would receive the allocated Shmita Set-Aside as payroll or in a lump sum payment at the start of her individual sabbatical. Shmita accounts would be transferable, adapting to the mobile nature of modern employment. Staggered Shmita periods would minimize the impact on employer operations. At the same time, if even half of all employers elect to compensate for production lost to employees on hiatus, the Shmita cycle would pump over 4.5 million compensatory job opportunities into the economy.

Refreshing the Generational Playing Field

According to Torah, the Jubilee (Yovel) is observed once every fifty years. While many of its laws parallel those of the Shmita, one is unique: the requirement to repatriate property to its original owner at each Jubilee. It is perhaps the most radical economic concept in the lexicon of Jewish law.

The groundwork for property repatriation during the Yovel begins with a census. Numbers 25:10–30 describes the head count of the Hebrew tribes as they are poised to enter and conquer Canaan:

> Take a census of the whole Israelite community
> from the age of twenty years up, by their ancestral
> houses, all Israelites able to bear arms. (Numbers
> 26:2)

Although the initial purpose of the census was to assess the strength of the Israelites for the approaching campaign of conquest, it also guided the apportionment of a land grant to each

Hebrew family. The land grant was determined by lottery, not by status or piety. Every head of household received the same share.

> Among these shall the land be apportioned as shares, according to the listed names: with larger groups (from the census) increase the share, with smaller groups reduce the share . . . Each portion shall be assigned by lot. (Numbers 26:53–56)

Every fifty years, without regard to the economic swings and transactions of the interim period, land and housing outside walled cities reverted to their original owners. The entire concept of "proclaiming liberty throughout the land," enshrined on the Statue of Liberty, was linked to thoroughgoing property repatriation.

> You shall hallow the fiftieth year. You shall proclaim release throughout the land for all its inhabitants. It shall be a jubilee for you: each of you shall return to his holding and each of you shall return to his family. (Leviticus 25:10) . . . In the jubilee year the land shall revert to him from whom it was bought. (Leviticus 27:24) . . . But houses in villages that have no circling walls shall be classed as country; they may be redeemed, and they shall be released through the jubilee. (Leviticus 25:31)

Probably in recognition of the investment people made in their family residences, the Jubilee laws made an exception for a personal home. If a house within a city was sold by the original owner of the land grant, his right to reclaim the property from the buyer lapsed after one year, the Jubilee notwithstanding.

> If a man sells a dwelling-house in a walled city, it may be redeemed until a year has elapsed since its sale . . . If it is not redeemed before a full year has elapsed, the house in the walled city shall pass to the purchaser beyond reclaim throughout the generations; it shall not be released in the jubilee. (Leviticus 25:29–30)

The Ancients required the return of the Hebrew land grant to its original owners once in the space of every two or three generations. Those who acquired the land in the interim still profited from its use. But the Jubilee limited the timeline of those who had acquired the property during the previous fifty years to bequeath it to their progeny. After two or three generations, the returned property re-leveled the economic playing field for original grantees and their descendants, giving them a fresh economic start.

Despite the increasing concentration of wealth in modern economies, Western societies offer no similar initiatives to refresh economic opportunity from generation to generation. Wealth-based privilege and estate transfers within families have upended any semblance of a level transgenerational playing field. Economist Chuck Collins of the Institute for Policy Studies characterizes the situation like this:

> Imagine a ten-mile race in which contestants have different starting lines based on parental educa-

tion, income, and wealth. The economically privileged athletes start several hundred yards ahead
of the disadvantaged runners. Each contestant
begins with ten one-pound leg weights. The . . .
advantaged competitors pull ahead quickly. At
each half-mile mark, according to the rules, the
first twenty runners shed two pounds of weights
while those in the last half . . . take on two additional pounds. After several miles . . . an alarming
gap has opened.[124]

Collins suggests higher levels of investment in public
infrastructure to reduce these inherent advantages. Changing the
rules of intergenerational wealth transfer is a critical mechanism
to achieve the same end. Fifty percent of the aggregate US estate
value newly reported in 2012 was not subject to taxation. Less
than 7% of the total value of estates was captured under current
tax policy.[125]

In 2012, this system left about $116 billion with inheri-
tors who have themselves done nothing to earn it. In conjunction with significantly increasing business profits, this regressive
inheritance system obstructs the presentation of a level economic
playing field to successive generations.

The rights to bequeath and inherit present vexing issues.
Virtually all cultures value the concept of creating wealth to leave
behind for one's children. The Yovel likewise placed no historical
limitations on bequests for periods of up to fifty years. Like the
Yovel, the modern Just Market promotes the level playing field
now and for the future, including the preservation of transgenerational opportunity.

The very idea of repatriated property seems far-fetched in today's environment. And from the traditional religious perspective, whatever the values behind the Jubilee may be, they are for practical purposes mooted in the modern world:

> It is the accepted Rabbinic view that the Jubilee is bound up with the territorial integrity of the Jewish State on both sides of the Jordan; and that accordingly its observance came to an end with the cessation of the Hebrew polity.[126]

And yet, while the return of hard assets to original individual owners (whoever they may be and however they might be identified) would be a mechanically staggering undertaking in the modern economy, the economic ethic behind the Yovel—leveling the playing field to create new opportunity and remove unfair advantage from those who have not earned it—is as valid now as it was during the period it was conceived. Indeed, why should some toe up to the starting line with the huge advantage of inherited wealth, while others enter the economic arena with nothing? It is the antithesis of the entrepreneurial ethic.

An estate-transfer policy that supported Yovel values would acknowledge three conflicting human desires: to pass on accrued wealth to descendants; to reward wealth creators with the ability to pass on their assets; and to rebalance the playing field for each generation.

The current paradigm supports the first two of these values, but not the third. A *Yovel Transfer Reserve* would, beyond a specified threshold, reserve all *created* wealth to be passed on to two successive generations (more or less in line with the fifty-year

Jubilee interval) and then repatriate that wealth to the general populace through an annual distribution.

The mechanism for the Yovel Transfer Reserve could be relatively straightforward and use a simple tax-return tracking mechanism:

First, in keeping with the original Yovel exclusion of homes in walled cities from the Jubilee redistribution, an exemption, say half a million dollars, would be available to all estates. The exempt portion would transfer without tax liability to the Yovel Reserve Fund. Based on estate values newly reported in 2012, this homestead exemption would reduce the overall estate values of the Reserve by less than four billion dollars, a little more than 3%.

Created wealth over and above the exempt amount remains in the family of the wealth creator (or with other designated heirs) for two successive generations. Those generations also retain wealth they additionally create (from the inheritance and other sources) for themselves, their children, and grandchildren. As is currently the case, those inheritances may or may not be subject to immediate estate taxation depending on social policy requirements of the moment.

In the fourth generation, however (after retaining control of the wealth "in-house" for approximately fifty years), any non-taxed portion of the original inheritance is surrendered to the Yovel Reserve Fund. The mechanism creates a rolling reserve, replenished each year by a new wave of Yovel taxes from funds that have been "in-house" for three generations. The opportunity to utilize bequeathed funds to generate more wealth balances the tendency to squander the inheritance rather than lose the money to fourth-generation taxes.

By its nature, a fully funded Yovel Transfer Reserve mechanism would phase in over a period of about forty years. As the cycle of contributions is activated, the annual distribution from the Yovel Transfer Reserve would be more than $3,000 per US household in current dollars.[127] Future policy debates would determine whether the Fund would deposit Jubilee wealth in, as Chuck Collins suggests, an "'education-opportunity trust fund' to provide debt-free college educations for first-generation college students"[128] or directly invest it with US households. Either way, the original objective of "proclaiming liberty throughout the land" is fulfilled.

From Ethics to Advocacy

The most radical Just Market policies have lain in the archives for two thousand years—not because they were deemed too extreme, but because of the inability of the ancient economic structure to overcome unintended consequences, such as the reluctance of wealthy individuals to extend interest-free loans to farmers caught in the web of cyclical debt as the Sabbaticals approached.

The modern economic environment presents fewer constraints. Instead of personal lenders, the financial sector is now the source of almost all loans and cyclical debt. Rather than celebrating and rewarding the sector most responsible for hoarding profit and denying universal access to life's necessities, Just Market policies:

- *Establish credit card debt and payday loan cancellation cycles*, discouraging practices that profit from the overextension of personal assets for the benefit of the country's most profitable sector.

- *Rationalize interest rate regulation*, with a single national maximum rate that limits all financial instruments.

- *Implement meaningful freedom from indentured servitude through cyclical immigration reform* that liberates undocumented workers from their effective bondage every seven years.

- *Prohibit and meaningfully prosecute company store arrangements* designed to intimidate and further impoverish the working poor and undocumented populations in silence.

- *Advocate for an employer-funded Shmita Set-Aside that offers a universal three-month refreshment sabbatical* every seven years.

- *Promote a level transgenerational playing field by establishing a Yovel Transfer Reserve* that replaces current estate tax policies with a phased-in transfer of all estate assets to the public at the third bequest point.

7. CONCLUSION: VISION OR CHAOS

In his best-selling *The Price of Inequality*, Nobel laureate Joseph Stiglitz details an economic reform agenda designed to reinvigorate competition in the US and reduce the deepening economic inequalities felt by the vast majority of Americans. His approach is, quite naturally, that of the economist seeking to rationalize market forces in the interest of long-term growth and stability.

In *The Just Market*, I've repeatedly returned to Stiglitz and other liberal and progressive economists from the contemporary world. But why? Stiglitz alludes to Torah only once in his four-hundred-page book and the others not at all. And yet, in his final, prescriptive chapter in *The Price of Inequality*, Stiglitz calls for retooled public policies that curb fraud and excess profit, including efforts to make it more difficult for banks to "engage in predatory lending and abusive credit card practices." What he calls a "comprehensive attack" on our economic ills would include "stronger and more effectively enforced competition laws" and limits on the power of individuals to "divert so much of corporate resources for their own benefit." And he concludes that as a matter of righting its economic balance and moral compass, the US needs "a fiscal policy to maintain full employment—with equality . . . the most important government policy influencing well-being."[129]

It's hard to overlook the resonance between these views, which derive social morality from the practice of economics, and the conclusions reached by the very different route that begins with the identification of Just Market values and concludes with a program that represents them in the current era.

Here's the point: the Just Market is no mere collection of random, fantastical thoughts. Its foundations, and even the specific policies and mechanisms proposed throughout this volume, correspond in significant part to the findings of the best economists of our day, many of whom are cited in these pages. Some of them might cringe at the Talmudic association, but their words tell the story of enduring values from the Ancients, embodied in the Pe'ah set-aside, the constraint on excess profits, condemnation of commodity speculation, and the transgenerational justice embodied in the Yovel.

We've already quantified the benefits of Just Market values and policies. What are the costs? Even after the deductions for the Just Market set-asides discussed in this volume, every US economic sector remains in the black, most with healthy profits (table 7-1). Even after deducting the Pe'ah and Shmita set-asides, three sectors—mining, finance-insurance, and real estate–rental—all show enough profit after both set-asides to "qualify" for treatment under the Onah Portion mechanisms for excess profits.

In the preface I spoke about the alienation of Jews from community and religious leadership that has largely ceased to lead Jewishly around pressing social issues of our day, and noted the

Table 7-1. Projected 2010 Just Market Business Impacts ($Billion)

	Receipts	Total Expenses	Set-Asides		Net Income		Onah	
			Pe'ah	Shmita	Percent	Dollars	Percent	Dollars
Total	20,587	18,750	313	151	7.3%	1,372		88
Agriculture	122	112	2	1	6.3%	7		
Mining	303	247	4	2	20.1%	50	3.35%	8
Utilities	361	346	6	1	2.3%	8		
Construction	775	729	12	7	3.7%	27		
Manufacturing	5,879	5,359	89	33	7.4%	398		
Wholesale Trade	3,212	3,086	52	9	2.1%	66		
Retail Trade	2,801	2,692	45	12	1.9%	52		
Transport-Warehousing	558	529	9	7	2.6%	14		
Information	808	707	12	9	11.4%	80		
Finance-Insurance	2,602	2,140	36	17	19.1%	409	2.39%	51
Real Estate Rental-Leasing	211	152	3	3	35.3%	54	18.57%	28
Professional Services	875	788	13	17	7.3%	58		
Management of Companies	604	510	9	5	15.9%	81		
Administrative-Support-Waste Mgt.	364	339	6	9	3.2%	11		
Educational Services	56	48	1	1	12.6%	6		
Health Care-Social Assistance	533	487	8	11	5.3%	26		
Arts-Entertainment-Recreation	52	45	1	1	12.4%	6		
Accommodation-Food Services	325	300	5	5	5.2%	16		
Other Services	144	134	2	2	4.5%	6		

Percentages displayed as a portion of Total Expenses
IRS Corporation Source Book 2010; 2007 Economic Census

wisdom of Proverbs: "Without vision, the people become chaotic" (Proverbs 29:18).

Jewish advocacy for Just Market values addresses one part of that vision gap. Like much of Jewish tradition, the Just Market represents hope for a better, more generous future.

Just Market values are part of the four-thousand-year-old Jewish family album. Like any family album, ours has great pictures, terrible pictures, and snapshots we wish hadn't been taken in the first place. Each of us gushes or weeps over different sections of the album. But in its entirety, that album is ours. It offers us lessons from the past and tools for the future. Although the values it expresses are open for all to see and appropriate (or misappropriate, for that matter), this family album belongs to us.

The snapshots in our album depict religious practices, everyday life, and social policy. They describe slaves and free persons, love and cruelty. At many points, our album reflects the intolerance of ancient times. But at many more, it represents the highest aspirations of justice available to the peoples of an earlier era. We are the descendants of the Ancients who had the wisdom to create, expand, and pass this album on to us. We were "chosen" to receive the album and its teachings. We inherit the opportunity to probe the core values of our civilization and adapt them as the highest aspirations of justice available to the world of *our* time.

It's my hope that this modest examination of the roots of a market approach grounded in a Jewish view of equity will stir the debate about the relevance of our civilization to the great issues of modern times, and that for some it will spur a progressive Jewish contribution to the political climates in which Jews live. There have been and will be diminishing returns for a Jewish civilization that does not support, or does not consider it important to address, issues of economic equity, opportunity, and stability; to condemn fraud, support full employment and, of course, universal access to the necessities of life.

The pretense of unity in the face of deterioration, of higher spiritual meaning in the face of social deprivation, does our people no honor. Those who worry that the synagogue treasuries are too weak to open debate may be missing the real danger.

The Ancients teach: "You are not obligated to complete the work, but neither are you free to desist from it" (Pirkei Avot 2:21).

Appendix A.
Other Contemporary Views of the "Jewish Market"

Meir Tamari is the founder of the Center for Jewish Business Ethics and Social Responsibility in Jerusalem. He suggests that those who begin to search the ancient source texts with a political bias are likely to look for evidence to support their beliefs.

> It is extremely difficult for a scholar not to inject his or her own economic or religious philosophy into the discussion, yet that bias is not always made clear to the reader. So we find that in the first half of this (twentieth) century many studies were heavily influenced by the socialist or liberal philosophers of the time and tend, therefore, to present a Judaism synonymous with those philosophies. At the present time, the pendulum seems to have swung in another direction, and now scholars tend to equate Judaism with the most extreme free market philosophers.[130]

As Tamari notes, it's not subjectivity that causes a problem in the search for original values. Rather, it's the *concealment* of a preexisting point of view that poisons the inquiry. In real life, every analysis of Torah and Talmudic texts is shaped in part by the priorities and assumptions of the author (including this one).

The Just Market approach to the Jewish economic tradition is not objective. It creates a narrative that extracts enduring values from Torah and the Talmudic texts and adapts them to modern reality. The Just Market recognizes that some practices and beliefs that were accepted as a matter of course during the epoch of the Sages—indentured servitude, for example—have no legitimate place in the modern world. The selection of *which* values to apply (and exclude) naturally reflects a bias.

This approach to a Jewish view of economic justice is distinctly different than two others: the Halakhic Market approach of Orthodox Judaism, and another that could be best understood as a distinctively Jewish Free Market approach.

The *Halakhic* Market Approach

The entire flow of the *Halakhic* Market (literally "the path")[131] stems from the principle that the "Divine origin of wealth is the central principle of Jewish economic philosophy."[132] From this perspective, wealth ultimately belongs to the divinity; humanity is enjoined to use it in accord with divine law. To the significant extent that divine law (including the Oral Law, Talmud, and subsequent interpretations by Orthodox *poseks*, or legal decisors) calls for intervention in the marketplace, regulation is good. To the extent that regulation, or any other action, is neither promoted nor forbidden, the Halakhic Market approaches it with neutrality.

Thus, within the Halakhic Market approach, there is nothing wrong with advocating a particular economic system, as long as it is conditioned by the decisions of generations of Orthodox judges who have weighed in on business issues. Within this milieu, Orthodox economist Aaron Levine comments that "public policy provides an appropriate setting for an interface between economic theory and halakhah."[133]

Personal biases are as apparent in the writings of proponents of the Halakhic Market as much as anywhere else. For example, after acknowledging that "interfering with the natural workings of the marketplace for the purpose of promoting social welfare finds historical precedent in the Talmudic essential foodstuffs ordinance," Levine concludes that any such constraint is economically "self-defeating" and can be safely ignored.[134]

Meir Tamari also writes from a Halakhic perspective. He emphasizes the importance of the economic sphere in Jewish law, pointing out that "of the 613 Divine commandments mentioned in the Torah, well over 100 are related to it."[135] Tamari's approach to the Halakhic Market frequently comes to conclusions similar to those of the Just Market outlook. He not only agrees that "market forces must be constrained by consideration of justice and righteousness," but also that "the regulation of prices, profits and competition was a legitimate concern of rabbinic courts."[136] Levine, with notably less enthusiasm, often signs on, though with an inclination to minimize the impact of prior religious rulings that Tamari cites to support his analysis.[137]

Aside from the rather significant requirement of a divine ideology, the Halakhic Market maintains two major points of difference with the Just Market approach. The first is its structural basis, including the belief that the chain of recognized rabbis who have looked at economic issues over the generations are imbued with a divine authority that cannot be questioned: Here is Tamari's observation:

> The legal structure of Judaism has at all times rested primarily on its Divine origin and on its moral claim on the Jew . . . Since the chain of tradition stretches back to the revelation at Sinai, the further back in time a source goes, the greater the legal authority attributed to that source. This means that the *Amoraiyim* cannot reject a ruling of the sages of the Mishnah.[138]

Just as the later fourth- and fifth-century rabbinical Sages known as the Amoraiyim cannot contradict rulings of the earlier Mishnah, no matter the social context, generation after generation of rabbinic scholars can carve additional constraints into Orthodox law without considering whether the conditions that led to an original ruling still apply.

This approach may be entirely satisfactory to Orthodox Jews, but it is ill-suited to most moderns, who are unlikely to get cozy with the exclusive hierarchy of rabbinical decision makers that govern the development of new law. Nor is it designed to have any real-world impact in the societies (outside of Israel) in which Jews live.

The second dividing line is methodological. The Halakhic Market builds, step by step, on Torah, Talmud, and successive commentaries on a case-by-case basis. It is a legal approach that prides itself on the clear, straight lines from divine commandment to civil law, but shies away from its implications for rapidly changing contemporary realities. As a result, despite the professions of policy interest from luminaries such as Aaron Levine, many important biblical value implications are ignored. The Halakhic Market has built a raft of significant commentary around issues of fraud in the marketplace, for example, because many of the conditions that produce fraud, and its reflections, are not dissimilar to what they were two thousand years ago.[139] But where conditions change radically, the Halakhists are reluctant to extract values and reengineer specific applications. Rather, the values themselves are effectively discarded.

The Sabbatical Year (Shmita) values of Jewish law provide a good illustration. The Orthodox view is that the Sabbatical Year values concerning debt forgiveness are mooted by the two-thousand-year-old Prosbul compromise—regardless of the need to address crushing modern debt cycles and the vast changes in the nature of lending. Its proponents would also contend that the economic values of the Jubilee Year, the "Sabbatical of Sabbaticals," were made irrelevant by the destruction of the second Temple.[140] This would seem to reduce to a historical curiosity Tamari's acknowledgement that "one explanation" for the laws of the Jubilee was "to prevent the accumulation of land by a small, monopolistic group of people." Elsewhere he notes that "many . . . biblical scholars" describe Jubilee practices as "a means of reducing social tensions between rich and poor."[141]

Monopoly power is certainly a concern for modern societies as well. But even if Tamari were to personally support the modernization of Sabbatical and Jubilee laws, the straitjacket of halakhah constrains him from advocating around either *as a Jewish issue.* By contrast, the Just Market examines the implications of both Sabbatical and Jubilee *values* for application in Israel and elsewhere, for today as well as the era of the Temple.

A contemporary Just Market approach respects the historic devotion of halakhah to assessing and maintaining a system of economic practices, but declines to settle for the general unwillingness of the Orthodox hierarchy to creatively update ancient sources to pressing modern social demands. Just Market values do not require the harness of Orthodox Jewish law.

The Jewish Free Market Approach

Where the Halakhic Market approach considers Talmudic texts in the light of historical practices as well as halakhah, the Jewish Free Market accesses halakhah and other ancient sources in full-throated support of unbridled capitalism.

Yosef Yitzhak Lifshitz, a Fellow at the Shalem Center in Jerusalem, is representative of a Jewish Free Market approach. Like both the Halakhic and Just Market approaches, Lifshitz seeks confirmation for his economic views in Talmud and the tradition. He summarizes his premise in an essay published in 2004:

> . . . (T)his popular identification between Judaism and socialism is a false one . . . (T)he two central ideas, which sustain the socialist redistribution of wealth—the limitation of individual property rights and the dream of economic equality—are alien to both the laws and spirit of Judaism as reflected in the Hebrew Bible and the rabbinic tradition.[142]

Lifshitz tries to demonstrate that socialist ideology is rooted in Christianity while unrestricted property rights are grounded in core Jewish values. He concludes that "the right to private property in Judaism is nearly absolute, and can be restricted in only the most extreme circumstances." He argues that property rights even extend to neglect and destruction: "As opposed to the classical Christian view, the property of the wealthy in Judaism is entirely theirs, to do with as they wish."[143] In his later work *Judaism, Law and the Free Market* (Acton Institute, 2012), Lifshitz focuses on personal charitable responsibilities, rather than market regulations and constraints, as the source of market obligations found in Jewish source texts. Talmudic regulations (profit constraint and pricing regulation) are characterized as mere holdovers from Roman practices. Inaccuracies aside, this view of a set of Sages so influenced by pagans seems an odd perspective from an Orthodox commentator.

A sympathetic view is advanced by economists Corinne and Robert Sauer in their 2012 *Judaism, Markets and Capitalism* (also published by the Acton Institute, which describes itself as "related" to the right-wing Heritage Foundation website). The Sauers identify five "axioms . . . of Jewish economic theory": participation in the creative process; protection of private property; accumulation of wealth; caring for the needy; and limited government. Not a single mention of Talmudic market constraints on prices, profit, or speculation appears anywhere in their thirty-two-page essay, which, through example of the priestly Temple tithe, also claims the flat tax as illustrative of Jewish economic theory.

As we've seen, these free market views are simply not consistent with the source texts or the tradition. From the proponents of the Halakhic Market, we know that prices, profits, and competition are all subject to regulation in Jewish tradition and law. We know from the discussion of gleaning in the Mishnah that a property owner who withholds gleanings, or gives favored access to one at the expense of another, or obstructs gleaning activity in any way is guilty of theft—not just of being unchari-table or morally deficient.[144] Meir Tamari supports the view that gleaning laws represent a right of the poor (and not only the Jewish poor), and are not voluntary charity in its traditional Christian sense:

> The poor have the *right* to participate in the Jewish farmer's harvest . . . If the poor do not wish to avail themselves of the bounty . . . then (it) becomes available to everyone. (Italics added)[145]

Lifshitz explains this contradiction by noting that the gleaning laws are classified as religious, rather than civil law—and so they escape his definition of behavior coerced from property owners, even when (as here) corporeal punishment is mandated in the ancient texts for those who obstruct the gleaning process.[146]

We also know from the plain language of Talmud that a property owner who digs a pit accessible to the public is liable for damages if a person or animal falls in it and sustains injury.[147] As well, a landlord has the responsibility to "erect doors, make the windows, strengthen the ceiling, and support the joists" whether he wants to or not.[148] It's hard to reconcile these and the long list of other property constraints with Lifshitz's notion that Jewish law is free of them.

The biggest problem with the Jewish Free Market

approach, however, is the socialist bogeyman it constructs. It's certainly true that Jewish socialists have in the past tried to equate their ideology to the tradition, and some of those left standing no doubt still do. (I myself have been guilty of that at earlier points in my life.) But Lifshitz and others scare up this straw man as a foil against Jews who search the tradition for progressive values of any sort. There is a vast gulf between asserting that Jewish values do not advocate socialism and asserting that Jewish support of private property rights are virtually absolute.

Appendix B.
The Just Market and the Gospels

Both Jesus and the Apostle Paul lived in the period just before the destruction of the second Jewish Temple—a time of national insurrection and religious upheaval in the Jewish community. Externally, Jewish militants in Palestine engaged Rome in ill-fated rebellion. Internally, debate raged over issues of interpretative versus literal law, the afterlife, and the Prosbul debt law compromise. The economics of debt triggered resentment, including the burning of debt records (chronicled by Josephus in *Bellum Judaicum*) and playing a role in the revolt that began in the year 66 of the Common Era and that culminated in the sacking of Jerusalem.[149]

During his life, Jesus criticized supporters of the Jewish Oral Law (the Pharisees) as hypocrites and oppressors. But whatever Jesus (and Paul) thought of day-to-day Pharisaic behavior, they also supported the movement as the standard-bearer for an evolving view of divine law that valued interpretative human development and rejected narrow readings of the Written Law (which were generally promoted by the Temple priesthood).

Asserting his Jewish bona fides, Paul made his allegiance clear in the ongoing struggle between the Temple caste and the Pharisee supporters of the Oral Law: "Concerning the Law," he says, "(I am) a Pharisee" (Philippians 3:5). Jesus notes approvingly that the Pharisaic outlook is consistent with Torah and a complement to it. He bids his followers to listen to Pharisaic teachings:

> Then Jesus said to the crowds and to his disciples: "The scribes and the Pharisees sit in Moses' seat. Therefore whatever they tell you to observe, that observe and do, but do not do according to their works; for they say, and do not do. (Matthew 23:1–3)

By guiding his disciples to "do whatever they (Pharisees) teach you and follow it," both Jesus and Paul align themselves foursquare with the Oral Law. While they specifically critique aspects of Jewish practice such as dietary laws (*kashrut*) and Sabbath observance, they never dispute economically-based Torah commandments or their expansion in the Oral Law. On the contrary, centerpiece teachings of the Christian testament are directly linked to Just Market values and source texts.

Some Christian scholars have taken note of correspondence between early Gospel values and Torah-based Just Market concepts. In a discussion of Mark 12:28–34, theologian Richard Horsley references what he terms the "greatest commandment" (to love one's neighbor), noting that ". . . the earlier generations of priests and scribes who had edited the Holiness Code knew that 'love your neighbor'. . . functions here as a summary of a whole series of covenantal injunctions to leave crops in the fields for the poor to glean, not to steal or deal falsely."[150] Referring to Mark 14:24, Horsley concludes that "the covenant renewal at the center of the renewal of Israel is focused on economics,"[151] and that "Matthew's Jesus is demanding from those who have received the blessings of the new deliverance (that there should be) rigorously disciplined justice in social-economic relations, a justice that surpasses that of the scribes and Pharisees."[152]

Likewise, one of the most well-known parables of the Christian Testament and one of its most familiar of prayer passages both indicate direct links to Just Market values from the Jewish source texts.

The Workers in the Vineyard

In the parable of the Workers in the Vineyard (Matthew 20:1–16), an employer hires laborers at five intervals stretching over eleven hours of the same day. At each interval, the landowner spots a group of idle workers and tells them to go into his fields and begin work, no matter how late in the day he comes upon them. He conveys to each group the message he gives explicitly to the first set of late starters: "You also go into the vineyard, and whatever is right I will give you" (Matthew 20:4). At the end of the day, the vineyard owner instructs his foreman, "Call the laborers and give them their wages, beginning with the last to the first" (Matthew 20:8).

Regardless of what hour they began to work over the course of the day, each of the field hands is then paid a full day's wage, causing complaint among those who had labored since the morning: "These last men have worked only one hour, and you made them equal to us who have borne the burden and the heat of the day" (20:12). The landowner scoffs at their irritation.

> Friend, I am doing you no wrong. Did you not agree with me for a denarius? . . . I wish to give to this last man the same as to you. Is it not lawful for me to do what I wish with my own things? Or is your eye evil because I am good? So the last will be first, and the first last. (Matthew 20:13–16)

The traditional "Kingdom of Heaven" reading of any parable focuses on divine power (the landowner) to act unknowably and unimpeachably. It promises that those who accept Jesus and enter into the Kingdom of Heaven—even those who are saved late in the day (here the idle workers)—are as fully rewarded as those who did so from the first days of the messiah's appearance on earth. The fruits of their salvation are identical.

But the parables were also designed to resonate with the audience that received them. For the parable to succeed, first-century Jews had to identify with both the scenario and the earthly values it illustrated. Examined through that earthly lens, the parable of the Workers in the Vineyard showcases Just Market values.

First, the parable envisions the vineyard (the surrogate of the Kingdom of Heaven) as a place in which all who want employment will have it, no matter how long or how often it has been denied in the past. The vineyard owner offers work to successive groups of idle day laborers, even as the day wears on:

> "Why have you been standing here idle all day?"
> They said to him, "Because no one hired us." He

said to them, "You also go into the vineyard, and whatever is right you will receive." (Matthew 20:6–7)

Every idle group, no matter what its ability to contribute to the landowner's needs in what is left of the shrinking day, is given the opportunity to labor and be compensated. And every worker in every group accepts the offer willingly, fulfilling his end of the universal employment opportunity bargain. To first-century ears, this exchange surely corresponded to the ethic advocated by the Oral Law and later codified as Mishnah Pe'ah.

Second, the parable, like the ethics of Torah and the Talmud discussed in chapter 5, adheres to the Just Market rules of timely and respectful compensation. The parable is explicit that all of the laborers are paid promptly at the end of the day, just as Leviticus 19:13 and Deuteronomy 24:15 require: "Call the laborers and give them their wages, beginning with the last to the first" (Matthew 20:8). Elsewhere in the Christian Testament, the disciples are reminded that "the laborer is worthy of his wages" (Luke 10:7). And James echoes Deuteronomy 24:15 ("... he will cry to the Lord against you and you will incur guilt ...") when he condemns employers who abuse the labor relationship and deny timely wage payment:

Indeed the wages of the laborers who mowed your fields, which you kept back by fraud, cry out; and the cries of the reapers have reached the ears of the Lord of Sabaoth. (James 5:4)

Just as the rabbis of the Talmud inveighed against "great men" who despised the dignity of labor, the Christian Testament applies the same value as a metaphor for its savior himself: "For this One has been counted worthy of more glory than Moses, inasmuch as He who built the house has more honor than the house" (Hebrews 3:3), echoing both the ethic and the laws of Just Market labor relations.

Finally, the parable of the Workers in the Vineyard suggests that those who were able to work for only a few hours due to circumstances beyond their control should be rewarded as if they had labored the day long. Their compensation completes the Kingdom of Heaven interpretation of the parable. This final twist complicates its earthly mirror by highlighting a vineyard owner who is improbably willing to pay a full day's wages for a partial day's work.

As many Christian teachers have noted, the twist in the parable is what makes the Kingdom of Heaven interpretation work as a story. But what earthly experience permitted first-century Jews to recognize this unlikely twist in their own worldview? The answer is—the most basic foundation of the Just Market; that the Kingdom of Heaven would be a place in which those who struggled to find work would still be compensated with "the necessities of life" (made possible in the parable by payment of "what is right," reflecting the ideal of the "just wage"). In a passage that is often misappropriated by conservatives to condemn the lazy, 2 Thessalonians implies the same point: "If anyone will not work, neither shall he eat" (2 Thessalonians 3:10). The passage refers to Christian salvation; but its real point is that one who *is* willing to work *shall* eat (that is, will attain salvation). And if that labor and its reward are to be meaningful by virtue of the endeavor and not its timing, then that element of the story was likely intended to be taken in the broader Just Market sense of sustenance—*d'varim sheyesh ba'hen khayay nefesh*, "the necessities of life," available to all.

The Lord's Prayer

Whether their exposure was in a church or (for those of a certain age) in a public school, Christians and Jews alike in the US are familiar with the Lord's Prayer:

> Our Father who art in heaven, hallowed be thy name.
> Thy kingdom come, Thy will be done,
> On earth, as it is in heaven.
> Give us this day our daily bread.
> And forgive us our trespasses,
> As we forgive those who trespass against us.

In context, the prayer reflects Jesus's response when he was asked by his followers how to pray. It is clearly addressed to the divinity ("Our Father") and asks for an earthly experience that replicates a heavenly or "Kingdom" experience in which justice and mercy prevail. That experience is epitomized by three things: receiving "our daily bread," forgiving "our trespasses," and forgiving "those who trespass against us."

To the ancient sensibility, "bread" in a prayer-like context likely meant more than the literal loaf, signifying a broader view of sustenance and probably referring to a bundle of needs, just as it did in Moses's final charge to the Israelites in Deuteronomy 10:18, where "bread and clothing" are clearly buzzwords for "the necessities of life" that the Israelites were required to provide to the widow and the alien. By the first century, Jewish understanding of how things *should* be had been influenced by the Pharisee belief in *olam ha'bah* or the world-to-come. In it, the necessities of life would, of course, be provided to all—daily, as the Lord's Prayer iterates—referring to the just future world by the messianic phrase "thy kingdom come."

Three lines later, the popular translation asks to "forgive our trespasses." But, modern phraseology notwithstanding, the word "trespass" does not appear in the original prayer. Luke, who is widely believed to have been a non-Jew and who preached with Paul to the gentile nations, uses the word "sin" in his version of the prayer. But the earlier version in Matthew instead refers to monetary obligations: "And forgive us our debts, as we forgive our debtors" (Matthew 6:12). Rather than a generalized prayer asking for sin forgiveness, then, this section of the Lord's Prayer focuses very specifically on earthly economic activity—the Just Market Sabbatical value of debt forgiveness.

The Gospels were preached and then codified during the early implementation of the Prosbul, which effectively ended the requirement for debt forgiveness in the Sabbatical Year. The revision of the law was controversial among the early rabbis and, historical evidence suggests, among the Jewish peasant masses. How could it have been otherwise? Jewish social policy was in a trap of its own making. The Sabbatical laws required debt forgiveness, which reduced the number of those willing to lend as the seventh year approached. The Prosbul effectively ended that legal requirement in the hopes of spurring loans to tide over small farmers. Sometimes it worked as intended; at others the Prosbul merely served as an unwitting means for landowners to entangle the law's intended beneficiaries, the poor, who lost their land grants as their debts piled up.

In this context, the Lord's Prayer appears to uphold the virtue of debt forgiveness even though the practice had lost the force of law. Along with the rabbis, Jesus continued to promote lending to the poor. He does not weigh in on the Prosbul itself; his words simply support the Sabbatical economic values that it attempted to mediate.

The same focus on extending and forgiving debt is emphasized elsewhere in the Gospels. In Mark, the trap of cyclical debt is condemned by reference to the prophet Isaiah's plaint against those who "devour widows' houses" and appropriate their fields (Mark 12:40). In Luke's version of the Sermon on the Mount (sometimes called the Sermon on the Plain), Jesus challenges his audience: "Give to everyone who asks of you. And from him who takes away your goods do not ask them back . . . But love your enemies, do good and lend . . . and your reward will be great" (Luke 6:30, 6:35).

The two concerns that the Lord's Prayer uses to illustrate "how to pray" (receiving the necessities of life and forgiving debt) are economic. Both correspond to Just Market values in terms easily understood by the Jewish population *because both were already in the lexicon of the Law as it was commonly understood.*

Appendix C.
Onah Industry Estimate Detail

This table displays all thirty-nine industries for which an excess profit (Onah) portion is indicated by IRS corporate data in the years 2007–2010.

The Onah values here are displayed without regard to the Pe'ah Set-Aside (chapter 2) and the Shmita Set-Aside (chapter 6). In the full Just Market work-out shown in chapter 7, Onah is calculated only after deductions have been made for both Pe'ah and Shmita Set-Asides.

As noted in chapter 1, the four-year range of Onah values is very likely understated for three reasons: Only corporate data is included, while that of highly profitable partnerships and limited liability corporations is not; some high-profit industry segments are not broken out in publicly available IRS tables, obscuring their Onah profits with broader industry totals; and some firms in every industry perform far under Onah profit levels, so that the percentages of those firms that do surpass the "excess" profit level generate even higher returns than are shown (all of which would be subject to excess profit regulations).

Table C-1. Onah Portion Excess Profits 2007—2010 ($Billion)

	2007	2008	2009	2010	Total
Oil-Gas Extraction	9.6	10.1		3.2	22.9
Metal Ore Mining	1.0	5.3	6.0	12.3	24.6
Support Activities for Mining	5.4	1.3	0.5		7.2
Soft Drink-Ice Manufacturing			0.5		0.5
Breweries			1.0		1.0
Tobacco Manufacturing	11.4	7.9	1.7	1.2	22.3
Pharmaceutical-Medicine Manufacturing	1.5	1.7	34.0		37.1
Soap-Cleaning-Toilet Preparations		2.1		7.1	9.2
Semiconductors-Other Electronic Components	0.8	0.2		1.0	2.1
Wholesale Electronic Markets-Agents-Brokers				0.0	0.0
Pipeline Transportation	0.6				0.6
Periodical Publishers	0.0				0.0
Book Publishers	1.6				1.6
Software Publishers	7.7	3.9	6.0	8.3	25.9
Data Processing-Hosting-Related		0.7			0.7
Other Information Services		1.5		1.3	2.8
Depository Credit Intermediation			5.5		5.5
Commercial Banking		0.3		6.0	6.3
Savings Institutions-Credit Unions		0.3	2.1	3.0	5.3
Credit Card Issuing-Other Consumer Credit		0.4			0.4
Real Estate Credit (Mortgage Bankers)		0.0	0.6	0.5	1.1
International-Secondary Financing		2.3	0.8	0.9	4.0
Loan Brokers-Check Clearing-Related	2.8	0.2	2.0	3.9	8.8
Investment Banking-Securities Dealing		1.4	11.3	5.9	18.6
Securities Brokerage		0.3	1.2	0.7	2.2
Commodity Contracts-Dealing-Brokerage	0.3	8.2	0.3	0.1	8.8
Securities-Commodity Exchanges	9.9	1.1	7.4	12.0	30.4
Insurance Agencies-Brokerages	3.3	0.3	0.2		3.8
Funds-Trusts-Other Financial Vehicles	441.4	11.5	237.6	247.3	937.8
Lessors-Buildings	16.6	12.3	8.9	29.1	67.0
Lessors-Miniwarehouses	25.8	1.0	7.1	4.9	38.8
Real Estate Agents-Brokers	0.5				0.5
Other Real Estate Activities	3.2		0.8	0.9	5.0
Commercial-Industrial Equipment Rental			0.4		0.4
Lessors-Nonfinancial Intangible Assets	0.7	0.7	1.3	1.3	4.0
Scientific Research-Development	0.0	1.9	2.3	2.7	6.9
Offices of Other Holding Companies	15.6	20.0	21.7	30.8	88.2
Other Arts-Entertainment-Recreation	0.6			0.5	1.1
Total	560.4	97.0	360.7	385.2	1403.3

(IRS Corporation Source Book; Excess profit calculations based on 16.7% maximum)

Endnotes

Preface

1   "Capitalism and the Jews," Milton Friedman, The Freeman, October 1, 1988, http://www.thefreemanonline.org/columns/capitalism-and-the-jews/.

2   Joseph Berger, "Milton Himmelfarb, Wry Essayist," *New York Times*, June 15, 2006.

3   Derived from CNN Exit Poll data (US Presidential Election), November 7, 2012.

4   Jewish voting percentages taken from Sandy L. Maisel and Ira Forman, eds., *Jews in American Politics* (Lanham, MD: Rowman & Littlefield, 2004), 153.

5   Anna Greenberg and Kenneth Wald, "Still Liberal After All These Years?," in *Jews in American Politics*, eds. Maisel and Forman (Lanham, MD: Rowman & Littlefield, 2004).

6   See the campaign site of Rabbi Shmuley Boteach at http://shmuleyforcongress.com/on-the-issues/, which echoes the Republican right and counsels government to "get out of the way."

7   Steven M. Cohen, "Workmen's Circle 2012 Social Activist Survey," Workmen's Circle/Arbeter Ring, 2012, Questions #15-#16-#19.

8   Jerry Z. Muller, *Capitalism and the Jews* (Princeton, NJ: Princeton University Press, 2010), 130.

9   Ibid., 131.

10   James Diamond, "The First Debate Over Religious Martyrdom," *Jewish Review of Books*, Summer 2013.

11   Kurt Andersen, "The Downside of Liberty," *New York Times*, July 4, 2012.

12   "Jewish Values Survey 2012," Public Religion Research Institute, Washington, DC, April 2012.

13   Dov Ber Borochov, "The Jewish Labor Movement," in *Nationalism and the Class Struggle* (Westport, CT: Greenwood Publishers, 1937), 178.

14   Letter in response to "Cheering U.N. Palestine Vote, a Synagogue Tests Its Members" *New York Times*, December 6, 2012.

15   Borochov, "The National Question," *Nationalism and the Class Struggle*, 144.

16   Translated by the author. The Jewish Publication Society translation (used for citations throughout much of this book) is rendered as "For lack of vision, a people lose restraint." In this instance, "restraint" does not quite present the sense of collective lack of purpose conveyed by the Hebrew *yiparah am*.

17   Berl Katznelson, "Revolution and Tradition," *Davar*, July 22, 1934.

18   Frank Bruni, "The Divine Miss M," *New York Times*, July 24, 2012.

Introduction

19   Mishnah Ketuvot 7:8.

20   The actual text uses the words "ephah," an ancient weight, and "shekel," a coin denomination.

21   Joseph Telushkin, *Jewish Literacy* (New York: William Morrow and Co., 1991), 149.

22   Yehuda Kurtzer, "Paradigms of Place" in *Havruta* 6 (Winter 2011), Shalom Hartman Institute.

23   Sanhedrin 16b.

24   Sanhedrin 20a.

25   Kidushin 21b.

26   Maimonides, *Laws of Kings*, 6–8. See also "Fighting the War and the Peace: Battlefield Ethics, Peace Talks, Treaties, and Pacifism in the Jewish Tradition," Michael J. Broyde, JLaw.com, accessed October 17, 2013, http://www.jlaw.com/Articles/war1.html.

27   The exception involves the Bar Kokhba rebellion of 135 CE against Roman rule. The revolt was backed by important early rabbinical thinkers, Akiva among them, who were slaughtered by the Romans. The rebellion was the last Jewish military activity on behalf of the Jewish people until the Zionist defense militias were established some 1,700 years later, followed by the resistance fighters of the Holocaust period and then the establishment of Israeli armed forces in 1948. In a different context, Jewish vassal tribes in Yemen battled Mohammed on behalf of their monarch in the seventh century.

28   Sanhedrin 91b. Almost a thousand years later Maimonides confirmed that on the day after the messiah arrives, the Jews should not expect any massive social change "or that there will be a change in the order of creation." (Maimonides, *Mishnah Torah*, Helot Meacham 12:1)

29   Bava Metzia 47b. More on Rav Khiyya bar Youssef's case in chapter 4.

30   Hershey Friedman, "The Impact of Jewish Values on Marketing and Business Practices,"*Journal of Macromarketing* 21, June 2001.

31   BT Berakhot 32a.

32   Pirkei Avot 2:21.

1. Access to the Necessities of Life

33   Underscoring the importance of straightforward dealings (and perhaps rewarding those who engage in business with complete honesty), Maimonides also opines that where a seller fully discloses the extent of his profit to the buyer, the constraint cannot apply: "Those who say, 'My profit is such and such an amount,' are not subject to the law of overreaching; even if one says, 'I bought this article for a sela and am selling it to you for ten,' it is legitimate." (Maimonides, *Laws of Sale* 14:1–2).

34   Consumer Price Index, US Bureau of Labor Statistics, 2007–2013.

35   Tali Heruti-Sover, "The Israeli Paradox: So Many Jobs, So Little Income," *Haaretz*, October 28, 2013.

36   That is, hoarders and speculators who attempt to manipulate market prices by artificially creating shortages or gluts in product.

37 Robert Pollin, *Back To Full Employment* (Cambridge, MA: MIT Press, 2012), 160.

38 The still more pithy end of the quote from Amos: "If only the new moon were over so that we may sell grain, the Sabbath so that we could offer wheat for sale . . . We will buy the poor for silver, the needy for a pair of sandals" (Amos 8:4–6).

39 Gretchen Morgenson, "Speculators Get a Break in New Rule," *New York Times*, September 25, 2011.

40 Justin A. Gillis, "A Warming Planet Struggles to Feed Itself," *New York Times*, June 5, 2011.

41 Morgenson, "Speculators."

42 Tim Jones, "The Greater Hunger Lottery: How Bank Speculation Causes Food Crises," World Development Movement (July 2010).

43 That is, since the Sages limited profit to one-sixth of total expenses (rather than calculating against revenue, per modern accounting), then profit equaled one-seventh of sales.

44 The commonly accepted intent here is a wholesaler.

45 Meir Tamari, *With All Your Possessions* (Northvale, NJ: Jason Aronson Inc., 1998), 88–89.

46 David Van Biema, "The Financial Crisis: What Would the Talmud Do?," *Time*, October 10, 2008.

47 Robert Kuttner, "The Post-Katrina Leadership Gap," *Boston Globe*, October 1, 2005.

48 Joseph Stiglitz, "The 99 Percent Wakes Up," *Daily Beast*, May 2, 2012.

49 A chapter 5 discussion of wage gaps in apples-to-apples work focuses on discrepancies within job categories.

It concludes that the Just Market would limit the gap between minimum pay and the standard for conscientious work in any given enterprise to about 25%.

50　Ziv Hellman, "Trying to Bridge the Wage Gap," *The Jerusalem Report*, December 10, 2007.

Jack Ewing, "Swiss Voters Decisively Reject a Measure to Put Limits on Executive Pay," *New York Times*, November 25, 2013.

51　US Census Bureau Median Household Income, Table H-8.

52　US Internal Revenue Service, *Corporation Source Book*, 2002 and 2010.

53　Lior Dattel and Hilda Weissberg, "More Than Half of Israelis Are Poor, or at Risk of Becoming Poor," *Haaretz*, October 16, 2013.

54　Paul Krugman, "Profits Without Production," *New York Times*, June 21, 2013.

2. Universal Employment Opportunity

55　The term in Hebrew, *ger*, literally means "foreigner" or "stranger."

56　That is, from neither inside the sickle or hand, nor on the outside, but precisely in between the two.

57　Pollin, *Back To Full Employment*, 145.

58　Because beans and grapes were also sold as both fresh and dried product.

59　As opposed to those brought down by shaking the tree, the more effective method applied for the landowner's harvest.

60　That is, 1/24 of a dinar worth of grapes, signifying that there is not enough left in the field to be worth saving for the gleaners.

61   Literally "righteousness" in Hebrew, and emphatically not "charity."

62   US Bureau of Labor Statistics, current Population Survey, Tables U-3, U-4, U-5, U-6, and "Employment Situation Summary," June 2013.

63   "Resource Data and Chart Pack," Chuck Collins and Sam Pizzigati, citing the Congressional Budget Office and US Census, www.inequality.org/income-inequality.

64   Thomas Piketty and Emmanuel Saez, "Top Incomes and the Great Recession: Recent Evolutions and Policy Implications," Paper presented at the 13th Jacques Polak Annual Research Conference, Washington, DC: November 8–9, 2012.

65   Robert Kuttner, "The Joys of Recession," *American Prospect,* April 24, 2012.

66   "Report on Survey of US Shipyard and Repair Industries," US Department of Transportation Maritime Administration, 2001, 16.

67   Although the pe'ah formula at first appears to penalize high-cost lower-margin industries, the incentives proposed in chapter 5 strongly encourage additional investment and expenditure in high-margin industries, which would consequently increase their "pe'ah portion."

68   Joseph Stiglitz, *The Price of Inequality* (New York: W.W. Norton, 2012), 278.

69   Bill Marsh, *New York Times*, September 4, 2011, reporting on study results from Robert B. Reich, University of California, Berkeley; "The State of Working America" by the Economic Policy Institute; Thomas Piketty, Paris School of Economics, and Emmanuel Saez, University of California, Berkeley; Census Bureau; Bureau of Labor Statistics; Federal Reserve.

70   Steven Greenhouse, "America's Productivity Climbs but Wages Stagnate," *New York Times*, January 13, 2013.

71   David Brooks, "Thinking for the Future," *New York Times*, December 9, 2013. See also: Glen Hubbard, dean of Columbia Business School and former director of the Council of Economic Advisors under President George W. Bush, *Marketplace*, February 28, 2008.

72   Paul Krugman, "Robots and Robber Barons," *New York Times*, December 10, 2012.

3. A Level Playing Field

73   Stiglitz, *The Price of Inequality*, 270–271.

74   The table is developed from data generated by four separately conducted studies: "Going Local: Quantifying the Economic Impacts of Buying from Locally Owned Businesses in Portland, Maine," Garrett Martin and Amar Patel, Maine Center for Economic Policy, December 2011; "Thinking Outside the Box: A Report on Independent Merchants and the Local Economy," *Civic Economics*, September 2009; "Local Works: Examining the Impact of Local Business on the West Michigan Economy," *Civic Economics*, September 2008; "The San Francisco Retail Diversity Study," *Civic Economics*, May 2007.

75   US Bureau of Labor Statistics, "Usual Weekly Earnings of Wage and Salary Workers, Second Quarter 2013."

76   Hila Weissberg, "Yawning Wage Gaps Point to Deep Discrimination in Israel's Labor," *Haaretz*, December 17, 2012.

77 "Facts on Executive Order 11246," US Department of Labor, Office of Federal Contract Compliance Programs (OFCCP).

78 Stiglitz, *The Price of Inequality*, 282.

79 Because a father would tend to use his position to maximize the son's gleanings at the expense of others.

80 See chapter 2.

81 Paul Krugman, "Little Is Level about US Playing Field," *New York Times*, January 8, 2012.

4. Commercial and Promotional Integrity

82 William Black, interviewed on *Bill Moyers Journal*, April 3, 2009.

83 Talmud includes many additional requirements for cleaning various weighted materials, as well as prohibitions on the use of specific metals as weights or astringents for cleaning them. See, for example, Bava Batra 89b.

84 David Saelman, "The Importance of Maintaining Proper Weights and Measures in Jewish Law," *Chidushei Torah*, NDS, 2010.

85 Kim Severson, "Under Many Aliases, Mislabeled Foods Find Their Way to the Dinner Table," *New York Times*, December 15, 2012.

86 Since there is no mention to the contrary, we can assume that Rav Khiyya's prices—both of them—were within the permissible profit margin for wholesale goods.

87 David Kocieniewski, "A Shuffle of Aluminum, but to Banks, Pure Gold," *New York Times*, July 20, 2013; Kevin Drum, "Goldman Sachs and the Aluminum Warehouses," *Mother Jones*, July 22, 2013.

88   Although similar examples can be seen by poking through most people's pantries, for purposes of verifiability the cited practices are from these sources:
Goofs, Glitches, Gotchas," *Consumer Reports*, November 2011; September 2012; May 2013.
Elizabeth Rosenthal, "Tests Reveal Mislabeling of Fish", *New York Times*, May 11, 2011.
Kirk Johnson, "Survey Finds That Fish Are Often Not What Label Says," *New York Times*, February 21, 2013.

89   A corollary is that investors who willfully turn a blind eye to propositions that are "too good to be true" are culpable as well if reasonable investigation would have revealed the truth. (Mishnah Ketuvot 7:8)

90   Jonathan Zell, "Harm, No Foul: Sunday Dialogue," *New York Times*, August 5, 2012.

91   Ibid.

92   Joe Nocera, "Financial Scandal Scorecard," *New York Times*, July 20, 2012.

93   Tim Lee, "The LIBOR Scandal and You," *US News & World Report*, August 12, 2012.

5. Respect for Labor

94   Jill Jacobs, *There Shall Be No Needy* (Woodstock, VT: Jewish Lights Publishing, 2009), 125.

95   The pick of the crop, having received the most sun.

96   See also Leviticus 19:13

97   Bava Metzia 83a, discussed later in this chapter, speaks to ethical obligations to compensate workers even when it is not necessarily required by law.

98 Lawrence Glickman, *A Living Wage: American Workers and the Making of a Consumer Society* (Ithaca, NY: Cornell University Press, 1997), 3.

99 "2013 Poverty Guidelines," US Department of Health and Human Services, January 24, 2013.

100 Mishnah Pe'ah 4:4.

101 Jonathan Zell, "Harm, No Foul," *New York Times*, August 4, 2012

102 A commentary on this Talmudic passage in the Soncino edition of the Talmud (Brooklyn, NY: Soncino Press, 1935) explains that olive and fig trees "have thick branches which afford a firm foothold," reducing the safety concern in those situations.

103 Jill Jacobs, *There Shall Be No Needy*, 119.

104 "Work Stress Survey" conducted by Harris Interactive on behalf of Everest College, as reported on Globe News Wire, April 9, 2013 (http://globenewswire.com/news-release/2013/04/09/536945/10027728/en/Workplace-Stress-on-the-Rise-With-83-of-Americans-Frazzled-by-Something-at-Work.html).

6. Sabbatical Values

105 J. H. Hertz, Commentary on "The Jubilee," in *Pentateuch and Haftorahs* (Brooklyn, NY: Soncino Press, 1960), 532.

106 Les Christie, CNN Money, May 24, 2012.

107 Eran Azran and Arik Mirovsky, "Mortgage Crisis Looming, Bank of Israel Warns," *Haaretz*, September 16, 2013.

108 Bill Marsh, *New York Times*, September 4, 2011.

109 Federal Reserve, "Report on Consumer Credit," July 2012; "Credit Card Charge-Off and Delinquency Rates," May 17, 2013.

110 Stiglitz, *The Price of Inequality*, 269–70; Sam Gustin (Interview), *Daily Finance*, October 22, 2010.

111 BizMiner, "US Industry Market Reports" release, June 2013.

112 Isador Grunfeld, *Shemittah and Yobel* (London: Soncino Press, 1972), 2.

113 Ibid.

114 Mosi Secret and William Rashbaum, "7-Eleven Owners and Managers Charged in Immigration Raids," *New York Times*, June 18, 2013.

115 Theodore Nik et al., "Chicago's Undocumented Immigrants: An Analysis of Wages, Working Conditions, and Economic Contributions," Center for Urban Economic Development, University of Illinois at Chicago, 2002.

116 "Latino Workers in South Face Rampant Abuse," Southern Poverty Law Center, 2012.

117 Ibid.

118 Israel Drori, *Foreign Workers in Israel.* (Albany, NY: SUNY Press, 2009), 133.

119 Jews outside of the Land were not prohibited from cultivation, but were also not permitted to eat produce grown inside the biblical borders of Judea and Israel during the *Shmita* year. Debt release was practiced among Jewish communities in the Babylonian diaspora.

120 Mitch Ginsburg, "Give It a Rest," *Jerusalem Report*, October 15, 2007.

121   Yossi Tsuria, *Shmita Blog*, http://blog.tapuz.co.il/shmita (in Hebrew). Tsuria's focus is on the Sabbatical Year and its modern application, but his logic regarding the broader application of agricultural laws of the Sabbatical apply equally to gleaning and other agricultural proofs discussed by the Ancients.

122   For a more culturally focused view of a modern Shmita vision, see Yossi Tsuria's entire Shmita blog at http://www.tapuz.co.il/blog/userblog.asp?FolderName=shmita&r=1 (in Hebrew).

123   Elizabeth and Barbara Pagano, "Time As the New Currency," accessed October 17, 2013, http://yoursabbatical.com/files/2009/08/TimeAsTheNewCurrency.pdf.

124   Chuck Collins, "The Wealthy Kids Are Alright," *The American Prospect*, May 28, 2013.

125   Internal Revenue Service, "Estate Tax Returns Filed in 2012."

126   J. H. Hertz, "Introduction to Seder Zerai'm," *Soncino Talmud*, 1917.

127   Internal Revenue Service, "Estate Tax Returns Filed in 2012."

128   Collins, "The Wealthy Kids."

7. Conclusion: Vision or Chaos

129   Stiglitz, *The Price of Inequality*, 269–282.

Appendix A. Other Contemporary Views of the "Jewish Market"

130   Tamari, *With All Your Possessions*, 9.

131   From halakhah, literally, the "path" or the "walk," used to denote the formal legal structure of Orthodox Jewish law.

132   Tamari, *With All Your Possessions*, 36.

133 Aaron Levine, *Economic Public Policy and Jewish Law*: (New York: Yeshiva University Press, 1993), 3.

134 Ibid., 24, 27–28.

135 Meir Tamari, *Sins in the Marketplace* (Northvale, NJ: Jason Aronson Inc., 1996), 14.

136 Tamari, *With All Your Possessions*, 86.

137 Levine, *Economic Public Policy*, 30–31.

138 Tamari, *With All Your Possessions*, 13, 17. The Amorayiim were the Sages of the fourth and fifth centuries who wrote the Gemara, the commentary on the Mishnah (Oral Law), which was itself the original commentary on Torah.

139 Tamari, *With All Your Possessions*, 44–48; *Sins in the Marketplace* (Northvale, NJ: Jason Aronson, 1996), 54–60; and Levine, *Free Enterprise and Jewish Law* (New York: Yeshiva University Press, 1980), 115–128.

140 See the detailed discussion in chapter 5.

141 Tamari, *With All Your Possessions*, 38. See also Tamari, *The Challenge of Wealth*, (Northvale, NJ: Jacob Aronson Inc., 1995), 23.

142 Yosef Yitzhak Lifshitz, "Foundations of a Jewish Economic Theory," *Azure* 5765, no. 18 (Autumn 2004).

143 Ibid.

144 Mishnah Pe'ah 5:6

145 Tamari, *With All Your Possessions*, 251–252 (italics added).

146 "Gleaning of the Fields," *Jewish Encyclopedia* (New York: Funk & Wagnall's, 1906), accessed October 17, 2013, http://www.jewishencyclopedia.com/articles/6704-gleaning-of-the-fields.

147 Bava Kama 50b

148 Bava Metzia 101b

Appendix B. The Just Market and the Gospels

149 Louis Feldman and Gohei Hata, eds., *Josephus, the Bible, and History* (Leiden, The Netherlands: Brill Leiden, 1988), 387.

150 Richard Horsley, *Covenant Economics* (Louisville, KY: Westminster John Knox Press, 2009), 130.

151 Ibid., 116.

152 Ibid., 131.

Index